JAI GURU DEV

CONCORDANCE
for the
BHAGAVAD-GITA

to be used with the

New Translation and Commentary

Chapters 1 - 6

by

MAHARISHI MAHESH YOGI

Prepared
by
CHARLES DONAHUE *and* DONNA SEIBERT

This work includes:

1) cross-referencing (e.g. enlightenment . . . see also fulfilment, realization)

2) reference to definitions of terms indicated by the abbreviation "df." before the page number

3) definitions of some Sanskrit terms included in parentheses following the term

4) an index of all analogies included at the end of the concordance (page 85)

5) some concepts listed in more than one way, e.g. "action, validity of" and also "validity of action" with full page references at each listing

6) both page numbers (for Penguin edition only) and chapter and verse numbers — this is so the Concordance can be used for both the paperback and hardcover *Bhagavad-Gita*

We hope you enjoy the Concordance and find it useful in as many ways as possible.

abandoned attachment, ch. 2 .. 135-138(v.48), 154-155(v.56), 157(v.57); ch. 5 .. 344-349(v.10-12), 352(v.14)

abandoning desire, ch. 3 .. 242(v.41); ch. 5 .. 370(v.23); ch. 6 .. 429-430(v.24)

ability to perform, ch. 3 .. 231-234(v.35)

ability to transcend, ch. 3 .. 207(v.15)

absence of desire, ch. 1 .. 51(v.28)

Absolute (see also Being, pure consciousness, transcendental consciousness), ch. 2 .. 79(v.2), 89(v.10), 94(v.15), 99(v.20), 104(v.26), 126-132(v.45), 169(v.68), 172(v.71); ch. 3 .. 177(intro.), 179(v.1), 192(v.8), 195-196(v.9-10), 198(v.11), 201(v.13), 205(v.14), 213(v.20), 215-216(v.22); ch. 4 .. 249(intro.), 125(v.1), 261-263(v.6-7), 265(v.9), 279(v.18), 307(v.35), 312(v.38); ch. 5 .. 339(v.7), 352(v.14), 354-355(v.15-16), 370(v.23); ch. 6 .. 391(v.3), 449(v.32)

Absolute and God, relationship of, ch. 6 .. 444(v.30)

Absolute and relative, junction-point of, ch. 6 .. 437-438(v.27)

Absolute and relative, relationship of, ch. 2 .. 95(v.15); ch. 3 .. 178-179(v.1), 183(v.3), 215(v.22); ch. 4 .. 307(v.35); ch. 5 .. 339(v.7), 344(v.10), 351(v.14), 356(v.16), 367(v.22); ch. 6 .. 442(v.29), 449(v.32)

Absolute, Incarnation of the, ch. 4 .. 261(v.6)

Absolute, nature of the, ch. 3 .. 188(v.5)

Absolute, power of the, ch. 4 .. 261(v.6)

absolute state of intellect, ch. 2 .. 140(v.49)

absolute state of knowledge, ch. 4 .. 312(v.38)

abstaining from action, ch. 3 .. 186-189(v.4-6)

abstinence from the activity of experience, ch. 3 .. 231(v.34)

abstract, ch. 2 .. 92(v.12), 102(v.24); ch. 3 .. 213(v.20), 241(v.40); ch. 4 .. 264(v.8), 290(v.23), 304(v.34); ch. 5 .. 328(intro.), 380(v.29); ch. 6 .. 420(v.18), 422(v.19), 467-468(v.47)

abstract and concrete desire, ch. 3 .. 241(v.40)

accomplished yogi, ch. 6 .. 402(v.10)

accomplishment of an action, ch. 4 .. 280(v.18)

Achyuta (Immovable), ch. 1 .. 42(v.21), 47(v.25)

action (see also activity), ch. 1 .. 62(v.37), 69(v.44), ch. 2 .. 80(v.3), 84-86(v.7), 100(v.21), 116-117(v.39), 118(v.40), 122-123(v.42), 125(v.44), 132-148(v.46-53); ch. 3 .. 178-181(v.1), 183-227(v.3-31), 231-234(v.35), 237(v.37), 239(v.39), 244-245(v.43); ch. 4 .. 250(intro.), 269-293(v.13-

25), 298(v.30), 300-304(v.32-34), 308-311(v.36-37), 314-315(v.38), 319-322(v.41-42); ch. 5 .. 328-336(intro.-v.5), 338(v.7), 341(v.7), 344-354(v.10-15), 365(v.21), 369(v.23); ch. 6 .. 384-387(v.1), 389-394(v.3-4), 400(v.8), 415(v.17), 429-431(v.24), 447(v.31), 466(v.46)

action, abstaining from, ch. 3 .. 186-189(v.4-6)

action, accomplishment of, ch. 4 .. 280(v.18)

action, aim of any, ch. 1 .. 62(v.37)

action aimed at reaching enlightenment, ch. 6 .. 466(v.46)

action and cosmic conciousness, relationship of, ch. 4 .. 290-292 (v.24)

action and renunciation, relationship of, ch. 5 .. 327-329(intro.)

action, annihilation of all, ch. 4 .. 309-311(v.36-37)

action, art of, ch. 2 .. 136-145(v.48-51); ch. 3 .. 226(v.30); ch. 4 .. 277(v.17)

action as means of liberation, ch. 3 .. 194(v.9)

action, attachment to (see also attachment), ch. 3 .. 217-220 (v.25-26)

action, authorship of, ch. 3 .. 200(v.12), 202(v.13), 221-223(v.27-28), 225-226(v.30); ch. 5 .. 345(v.10), 351-354(v.14-15)

action, beginning of (see also start of action), ch. 3 .. 206(v.15)

action, binding influence of (see also bondage), ch. 2 .. 115(v.38), 116-117(v.39), 142-143(v.50); ch. 3 .. 189(v.6), 194(v.9), 203(v.13), 218(v.28), 244(v.43); ch. 4 .. 274(v.16), 280-282(v.18-19), 319-321(v.41); ch. 5 .. 338-341(v.6-7), 347 (v.11), 370(v.23); ch. 6 .. 387(v.1), 398(v.6)

action, blessing of, ch. 3 .. 193(v.8)

action, cause of, ch. 2 .. 140(v.49)

action, code of, ch. 3 .. 186(v.3)

action, consummation of all, ch. 4 .. 301(v.32)

action, content of, ch. 3 .. 186(v.3)

action, desireless, ch. 3 .. 209(v.18)

action, disciplined, ch. 2 .. 122(v.42)

action, five factors for accomplishment of, ch. 2 .. 153(v.55)

action, five levels of, ch. 3 .. 212(v.19)

action, freedom of (see also free will), ch. 1 .. 63(v.39); ch. 2 .. 104-105(v.27); ch. 3 .. 180(v.1), 233(v.35); ch. 4 .. 268 (v.12)

action, fruit of, ch. 2 .. 133-135(v.47), 138-145(v.49-51); ch. 3 .. 199-200(v.12), df. 199(v.12), 225(v.30); ch. 4 .. 250(intro.),

271-272(v.14), 280-283(v.18-19), 285-286(v.20); ch. 5 .. 348-349(v.12), 351-354(v.14-15); ch. 6 .. 384-386(v.1)

action, fulfilment of, ch. 2 .. 134(v.47); ch. 3 .. 245(v.43); ch. 4 .. 268(v.12), 291(v.24), 310(v.37)

action, glory of, ch. 3 .. 205(v.14), 213(v.20)

action, goal of all, ch. 4 .. 302(v.33)

action, God's, ch. 3 .. 188(v.4)

action, good (see also right action), ch. 2 .. 111(v.34); ch. 5 .. 374(v.25)

action, impotence of, ch. 4 .. 301(v.32)

action-impression-desire, cycle of, ch. 2 .. 142(v.50); ch. 4 .. 284-286(v.19-20)

action in cosmic consciousness, ch. 3 .. 209-212(v.18-19), 217-227 (v.24-30); ch. 4 .. 278-292(v.18-24)

action in enlightenment, ch. 3 .. 217-218(v.25)

action in God-consciousness, ch. 6 .. 447(v.31)

action in ignorance, ch. 3 .. 217-218(v.25)

action, incentive to, ch. 6 .. 429-430(v.24)

action, influence of, ch. 2 .. 100(v.21), 137(v.48), 142-143(v.50); ch. 3 .. 197-198(v.11); ch. 4 .. 274(v.16); ch. 5 .. 350(v.13), 354(v.15)

action, knowledge of, ch. 4 .. 274-281(v.16-18), 308(v.36); ch. 5 .. 352(v.14)

action, man of, ch. 3 .. 184(v.3); ch. 6 .. 465-466(v.46)

action, mastery over, ch. 4 .. 291(v.24)

action, most highly refined, ch. 3 .. 193(v.8)

action, natural, ch. 3 .. 210-212(v.19), 229-230(v.33); ch. 5 .. 352(v.14)

action, nature of, ch. 4 .. 250(intro.); ch. 5 .. 330(v.1)

action, need for, ch. 2 .. 114(v.38); ch. 4 .. 268(v.12)

action of an enlightened man (see also characteristics of realized man), ch. 4 .. 281-292(v.19-24)

action of Krishna, ch. 3 .. 215-217(v.22-24); ch. 4 .. 264-265(v.9)

action on the sensory level, ch. 3 .. 183-184(v.3)

action, organs of, ch. 3 .. 189-190(v.6-7); ch. 4 .. 286(v.20), 315 (v.38); ch. 6 .. 429(v.24)

action, origin of, ch. 2 .. 140(v.49)

action, performance of, ch. 2 .. 118(v.40), 143(v.50); ch. 5 .. 327(intro.), 330(v.1), 346-348(v.11)

action, philosophy of, ch. 5 .. 327-328(intro.)

action, principle of, ch. 1 .. 69(v.44); ch. 6 .. 461(v.41)

action, process of, ch. 2 .. 134(v.47), 143(v.50); ch. 3 .. 191 (v.8); ch. 4 .. 278(v.18), 281-283(v.19)

action, purpose of, ch. 2 .. 114(v.38); ch. 3 .. 208-209(v.17-18), 212(v.19); ch. 4 .. 283(v.19)

action, purpose, start and progress of, ch. 4 .. 281-283(v.19)

action, quality of, ch. 4 .. 283(v.19)

action-reaction (see also *karma*), ch. 1 .. 63(v.39); ch. 2 .. 85 (v.7); ch. 3 .. 197-198(v.11); ch. 4 .. 267(v.11); ch. 6 .. 461(v.41)

action, result of, ch. 2 .. 115(v.38), 134(v.47), 139-140(v.49); ch. 3 .. 218(v.25)

action, right (see also good action), ch. 2 .. 84(v.7); ch. 3 .. 191-193(v.8), 200-203(v.13), 219-220(v.26); ch. 4 .. 276(v.17), 294(v.26), 296(v.27); ch. 6 .. 390(v.3), 427(v.23), 466 (v.46)

action, science of, ch. 3 .. 245(v.43); ch. 4 .. 280-290(v.18-23)

action, seed of, ch. 2 .. 143(v.50); ch. 4 .. 286(v.20), 311(v.37)

action, skill in, ch. 2 .. 141-143(v.50), 147-148(v.53); ch. 3 .. 190(v.7)

action, spontaneous right, ch. 3 .. 192(v.8)

action, stages of, ch. 2 .. 118(v.40)

action, start of (see also beginning of action), ch. 3 .. 213(v.20); ch. 4 .. 281-283(v.19)

action, success in, ch. 4 .. 250(intro.)

action surrendered to God, ch. 3 .. 226(v.30); ch. 5 .. 352-353 (v.14); ch. 6 .. 411(v.14)

action, theory of, ch. 3 .. 205(v.15)

action, thought of, ch. 3 .. 189(v.6)

action, upright, ch. 6 .. 459(v.40)

action, validity of, ch. 2 .. 114(v.38); ch. 3 .. 209-212(v.18-19), 215(v.22)

action, value of, ch. 2 .. 140(v.49); ch. 4 .. 276(v.17)

action worthy of performance, ch. 3 .. 210-212(v.19)

action, wrong (see also right and wrong, sin), ch. 1 .. 44(v.23); ch. 3 .. 191(v.8), 207(v.15), 220(v.26); ch. 4 .. 276-277 (v.17), 308-309(v.36)

action, Yoga of, ch. 3 .. 183-186(v.3), 189-190(v.7); ch. 5 .. 328-336(intro.-v.5), 365(v.21), 373(v.25)

actions, past, ch. 4 .. 259(v.5), 311(v.37)

activity (see also action), ch. 1 .. 51(v.28); ch. 2 .. 125(v.44), 128(v.45), 151(v.55), 158-159(v.58), 168(v.68), 172-174 (v.71-72); ch. 3 .. 179(v.1), 184(v.3), 186-190(v.3-7), 193 (v.8), 198(v.11), 200(v.12), 202(v.13), 204(v.14), 208 (v.17), 210-216(v.19-23), 219-221(v.26-27), 223(v.28), 225-229(v.30-33), 230-231(v.33-34), 233-235(v.35-36), 239-240(v.39-40); ch. 4 .. 250(intro.), 270-273(v.13-15), 276-284(v.17-19), 286(v.20), 292(v.24), 295-296(v.27), 298-299 (v.30), 301(v.32), 306(v.35), 309-310(v.36-37), 312-315 (v.38), 317-318(v.39), 320-322(v.41-42); ch. 5 .. 327-329 (intro.), 331-332(v.2), 337-342(v.6-9), 346-352(v.11-14), 361(v.19), 363-364(v.20-21), 369-370(v.23), 376(v.26); ch. 6 .. 384-387(v.1), 389-392(v.3-4), 406(v.12), 411-412 (v.14), 415-417(v.17), 425(v.21), 430(v.24), 434(v.25), 438(v.27), 446(v.31), 454(v.36), 466(v.46)

activity after meditation, ch. 3 .. 184-186(v.3), 194(v.9), 213 (v.20), 218-220(v.26), 226(v.30), 229(v.33); ch. 4 .. 292 (v.24), 312-314(v.38), 317(v.39), 320-322(v.41-42); ch. 5 .. 326(intro.), 335(v.4), 337(v.6), 344(v.10), 347-348 (v.11); ch. 6 .. 386(v.1), 391(v.3), 402(v.10), 436(v.26)

activity and Being, full stature of, ch. 5 .. 349(v.12)

activity and silence, ch. 4 .. 278-279(v.18), 282(v.19), 286(v.20), 313-314(v.38); ch. 5 .. 340(v.7); ch. 6 .. 392(v.3), 428 (v.23)

activity, basis of, ch. 3 .. 220-221(v.27); ch. 5 .. 341(v.7)

activity, direction of, ch. 4 .. 268(v.12)

activity, divine, ch. 3 .. 216(v.22); ch. 4 .. 264-265(v.9)

activity, external, ch. 6 .. 430(v.24)

activity, highest type of, ch. 3 .. 211(v.19)

activity, internal, ch. 6 .. 430(v.24)

activity, inward, ch. 3 .. 213(v.20); ch. 4 .. 292(v.24)

activity, levels of, ch. 4 .. 315(v.38)

activity, mental (see also thinking), ch. 3 .. 184(v.3), 189(v.6); ch. 4 .. 302(v.33), 315(v.38); ch. 5 .. 326(intro.), 335(v.4), 348(v.11), 369(v.23); ch. 6 .. 394(v.4), 434(v.25)

activity, most refined, ch. 3 .. 211(v.19); ch. 4 .. 313(v.38), 315 (v.38); ch. 5 .. 332(v.2), 348(v.11)

activity on the cosmic level, ch. 4 .. 279-280(v.18)

activity, outward, ch. 3 .. 213(v.20); ch. 4 .. 292(v.24)

activity, physical, ch. 5 .. 369(v.23)

activity, reduction of, ch. 4 .. 295(v.27)

activity, source of, ch. 3 .. 206(v.15)

activity, spur to, ch. 2 .. 128(v.45); ch. 3 .. 236(v.37); ch. 5 .. 349(v.12); ch. 6 .. 437-438(v.27)

activity, universality of, ch. 3 .. 188(v.5)

actor (see also doer), ch. 2 .. 142-143(v.50); ch. 4 .. 250(intro.), 276(v.17), 283(v.19), 310(v.37); ch. 5 .. 350-353(v.13-14)

actor, nature of the, ch. 4 .. 250(intro.)

adharma (absence of *dharma*), ch. 1 .. 64-66(v.40-41); ch. 4 .. 262-263(v.7)

advantages of *yagya,* ch. 3 .. 196-198(v.10-11)

after death, ch. 5 .. 375-376(v.26)

aggression, ch. 1 .. 36(v.13-14)

'aham tattva' (principle of mind), ch. 6 .. 424(v.21)

aim of any action, ch. 1 .. 62(v.37)

aim of Yoga (see also goal of Yoga), ch. 3 .. 177(intro.)

alertness, intellectual, ch. 4 .. 304(v.34)

alertness, restful, ch. 2 .. 168(v.68), 173(v.72); ch. 4 .. 313 (v.38); ch. 5 .. 346(v.11), 369(v.23); ch. 6 .. 393(v.3), 407(v.12), 417(v.17), 429(v.24)

all beings in the Self, ch. 4 .. 305-308(v.35); ch. 5 .. 338-341 (v.7); ch. 6 .. 441-442(v.29)

all beings seen in God, ch. 4 .. 307-308(v.35)

all knowledge, ch. 3 .. 228(v.32)

allotted duty (see also *dharma,* natural duty), ch. 3 .. 191-193 (v.8)

Almighty, power of the, ch. 3 .. 225-226(v.30); ch. 4 .. 263(v.7)

alone, ch. 6 .. 402-405(v.10)

analysis, ch. 2 .. 78(v.2), 152(v.55); ch. 6 .. 433(v.25)

anger, ch. 1 .. 46(v.25); ch. 2 .. 154-155(v.56), 163-164(v.62-63); ch. 3 .. 236-237(v.37); ch. 4 .. 265-266(v.10), 315(v.38); ch. 5 .. 368-370(v.23), 374-376(v.26), 377-378(v.28)

anger, departure of, ch. 2 .. 154-155(v.56)

animals, ch. 5 .. 358-360(v.18)

annihilation of all action, ch. 4 .. 309-311(v.36-37)

anticipation, ch. 6 .. 433(v.25)

anxiety, ch. 4 .. 286(v.21)

appreciation (see also enjoyment), ch. 5 .. 343-344(v.8,9); ch. 6 .. 433(v.25)

arguments, ch. 2 .. 78-79(v.2), 90(v.10), 103(v.26)

Arjuna, ch. 1 .. 31(v.4), 42-72(v.20-47); ch. 2 .. 76-91(v.1-11), 111(v.34), 127(v.45), 129-130(v.45), 146(v.52), 149-150

(v.54-55); ch. 3 .. 178-183(v.1-2), 214-215(v.21), 234-235 (v.35-36); ch. 4 .. 258-259(v.3-4), 306(v.35); ch. 5 .. 329-330(v.1), 380(v.29); ch. 6 .. 421(v.19), 451(v.34), 456 (v.37), 458(v.39)

art of action, ch. 2 .. 136-145(v.48-51); ch. 3 .. 226(v.30); ch. 4 .. 277(v.17)

art of being steady, ch. 6 .. 408(v.13)

artha (wealth, business, etc.), ch. 6 .. 427(v.23)

ascetic practices, ch. 5 .. 370(v.23)

aspirant to Yoga, ch. 6 .. 463(v.44)

Atman (transcendent Self) (see also Self), ch. 2 .. 98(v.18); ch. 5 .. 357(v.17)

Atmananda (Self-consciousness), ch. 4 .. 317(v.39); ch. 6 .. 428 (v.23)

attachment, ch. 1 .. 58(v.34); ch. 2 .. 135-138(v.48), 154-155 (v.56), 163-164(v.62-64), 172(v.71); ch. 3 .. 189-190(v.7), 193-195(v.9), 217-218(v.25), 224(v.29), 229-231(v.33-34), 233(v.35); ch. 4 .. 265-266(v.10), 281(v.19), 285-286(v.20), 288-289(v.23); ch. 5 .. 344-349(v.10-12), 356(v.16); ch. 6 .. 396(v.5), 453(v.35)

attachment, abandoned (see also detachment), ch. 2 .. 135-138 (v.48), 154-155(v.56), 157(v.57); ch. 5 .. 344-349(v.10-12), 352(v.14)

attachment and aversion, ch. 3 .. 230-231(v.34), 233(v.35), 236 (v.37); ch. 5 .. 362(v.20)

attachment to action, ch. 3 .. 217-220(v.25-26)

attainment, four levels of, ch. 6 .. 467(v.47)

attention, ch. 1 .. 53(v.29); ch. 2 .. 118(v.40), 134(v.47), 136 (v.48), 144(v.51); ch. 3 .. 194(v.9), 225(v.30); ch. 5 .. 376 (v.27); ch. 6 .. 409(v.13), 450-452(v.33-34)

attention, object of, ch. 3 .. 223(v.28); ch. 6 .. 436(v.26)

attribute, ch. 2 .. 102-103(v.24-25)

austerity, ch. 4 .. 265-266(v.10), 297(v.28); ch. 5 .. df. 379(v.29); ch. 6 .. 430(v.24), 466(v.46)

author of creation, ch. 4 .. 270(v.13)

authority of Krishna, ch. 4 .. 260(v.5)

authorship of action, ch. 3 .. 200(v.12), 202(v.13), 221-223(v.27-28), 225-226(v.30); ch. 5 .. 345(v.10), 351-354(v.14-15)

authorship of thoughts, ch. 6 .. 411(v.14)

automatic, ch. 2 .. 118(v.40), 162(v.61), 167(v.66); ch. 3 .. 190 (v.7), 198(v.11), 200(v.12), 225(v.30), 231(v.34); ch. 4 .. 262(v.7), 264(v.8), 276(v.17), 294(v.26), 296(v.27), 306

(v.35), 320(v.41); ch. 5 .. 332-333(v.2), 342-343(v.8,9), 345(v.10), 347(v.11), 361(v.19), 369(v.23), 374(v.25); ch. 6 .. 413(v.15), 417(v.17), 430(v.24), 440(v.28)

automatic *yagya,* ch. 3 .. 198(v.11)

aversion, ch. 2 .. 164(v.64); ch. 3 .. 230-231(v.34), 233(v.35), 236(v.37)

Ayurveda (the doctrine of health), ch. 4 .. 262(v.7)

balance of mind (see also evenness of mind, steady intellect), ch. 2 .. 135-141(v.48-49), 154(v.56), 164(v.63-64); ch. 6 .. 400(v.8)

balance in life, ch. 6 .. 400(v.8)

balanced breath, ch. 5 .. 376-377(v.27)

balanced in success and failure, ch. 2 .. 135-138(v.48)

balanced intellect (see also established intellect, steady intellect), ch. 2 .. 138-141(v.49)

balancing force of nature (see also equilibrium), ch. 1 .. 27-28 (v.1), 41-43(v.20-21); ch. 2 .. 108(v.31); ch. 3 .. 221 (v.27); ch. 4 .. 263-264(v.7-8)

basic principle of development, ch. 6 .. 395(v.5)

basis of all activity, ch. 3 .. 220-221(v.27); ch. 5 .. 341(v.7)

basis of all morality, virtue and right action, ch. 6 .. 427(v.23)

basis of equanimity, ch. 5 .. 361(v.19)

basis of God-consciousness, ch. 6 .. 452(v.34)

basis of nature, ch. 4 .. 284(v.19)

basis of right action, ch. 4 .. 294(v.26)

basis of the three *gunas,* ch. 3 .. 234(v.35); ch. 4 .. 270(v.13)

battle (also see fight, war, warrior), ch. 2 .. 109(v.32-33)

beginning of action (see also start of action), ch. 3 .. 206(v.15)

beginning of life (see also source of creation), ch. 3 .. 207(v.16)

behaviour, natural, ch. 3 .. 209(v.18)

behaviour of realized man (see also characteristics of realized man), ch. 2 .. 155-157(v.56-57); ch. 3 .. 209(v.18); ch. 4 .. 290(v.23); ch. 6 .. 401(v.9)

behaviour, righteous (see also good action, right action), ch. 1 .. 36(v.14), 63(v.39); ch. 6 .. 460(v.41)

behaviour, social, ch. 2 .. 110(v.33)

Being (see also Absolute, pure consciousness, transcendental consciousness), ch. 1 .. 43(v.21), 64(v.39); ch. 2 .. 81(v.3), 96-98(v.17-18), 100(v.21), 103(v.25), 115(v.38), 118(v.40), 127-129(v.45), 131-133(v.45-46), 136-137(v.48), 139(v.49),

142-144(v.50-51), 151(v.55), 159-160(v.58-59), 162(v.61), 164(v.64), 166(v.66); ch. 3 .. 179(v.1), 184(v.3), 186-188 (v.3-5), 190(v.7), 192(v.8), 194(v.9), 200-208(v.12-17), 213-214(v.20-21), 216(v.23), 218-219(v.26), 223-226(v.28-30), 230-231(v.33-34), 233-234(v.35), 238(v.38), 240(v.40), 243-244(v.43); ch. 4 .. 250(intro.), 253(v.1), 256(v.2), 259 (v.5), 261-262(v.6-7), 266-267(v.10-11), 270(v.13), 276 (v.17), 278-279(v.18), 283-284(v.19), 286-287(v.20-21), 291-297(v.24-28), 301(v.32), 303-304(v.34), 306-307(v.35), 309(v.36), 311-313(v.37-38), 320-322(v.41-42); ch. 5 .. 334(v.3-4), 337-341(v.6-7), 343-347(v.8-10), 349-352(v.12-14), 354-355(v.15-16), 359-361(v.18-19), 363(v.20), 368 (v.22), 370-372(v.23-24), 375(v.26); ch. 6 .. 386-387(v.1), 392(v.3), 394(v.4), 396-400(v.5-8), 402(v.10), 404-405 (v.10), 407(v.12), 410(v.14), 412-413(v.14-15), 418-419 (v.17-18), 423-424(v.20), 428(v.23), 430(v.24), 433-434 (v.25), 437(v.27), 440-445(v.28-30), 448(v.32), 450(v.33), 452-453(v.34-35), 455(v.36), 460(v.41), 462(v.43), 467-468(v.47)

Being and activity, full stature of, ch. 5 .. 349(v.12)

Being, infusion of, ch. 2 .. 144(v.51), 173(v.72); ch. 3 .. 211 (v.19), 214(v.20); ch. 4 .. 283(v.19), 291(v.24), 312-313 (v.38), 317(v.39); ch. 5 .. 340-341(v.7), 344(v.10), 350 (v.13), 363(v.20), 369-370(v.23); ch. 6 .. 386(v.1), 391 (v.3), 400(v.8), 405(v.10), 412(v.14), 436(v.26), 442 (v.29), 452(v.35), 462(v.43), 467(v.47)

Being, lack of, ch. 6 .. 450-451(v.33-34)

Being of the Lord, ch. 4 .. 260(v.5), 265(v.9); ch. 6 .. 414(v.15)

Being on the sensory level, ch. 2 .. 159-161(v.58-59); ch. 6 .. 443(v.30), 467-468(v.47)

Being, reflection of, ch. 2 .. 166(v.66)

Being, submission to, ch. 4 .. 304(v.34)

Being, thought of, ch. 5 .. 344-345(v.10)

beings, ch. 6 .. 461(v.41)

benefits of knowledge, ch. 4 .. 277(v.17)

beyond the intellect, ch. 3 .. 243-245(v.42-43); ch. 6 .. 425(v.21)

beyond the senses, ch. 6 .. 424-425(v.21)

beyond the *Veda,* ch. 6 .. 463(v.44)

Bhagavad-Gita, ch. 1 .. 49-52(v.28); ch. 2 .. 75(intro.), 81(v.3), 85(v.7), 116(v.39), 123-124(v.42), 127(v.45), 131(v.45); ch. 4 .. 252(v.1), 254(v.1), 256(v.2); ch. 5 .. 328(intro.), 377(v.27), 380(v.29); ch. 6 .. 383-384(intro.), 435(v.26), 443(v.29)

Bhagavad-Gita, essential wisdom of the, ch. 2 .. 117(v.39)

Bhagavad-Gita, glory of the, ch. 6 .. 441(v.28)

Bhagavad-Gita, history of the, ch. 4 .. 252-258(v.1-3)

bhakta (devotee of God), ch. 2 .. 86(v.7), 131(v.45)

binding influence of action (see also bondage), ch. 2 .. 115(v.38), 116-117(v.39), 142-143(v.50); ch. 3 .. 189(v.6), 194(v.9), 203(v.13), 218(v.28), 244(v.43); ch. 4 .. 274(v.16), 280-282(v.18-19), 319-321(v.41); ch. 5 .. 338-341(v.6-7), 347 (v.11), 370(v.23); ch. 6 .. 387(v.1), 398(v.6)

binding influence of desire (see also bondage), ch. 3 .. 239(v.39)

birth (see also born, cycle of birth and death), ch. 2 .. 103-104 (v.26-27), 143-145(v.51); ch. 4 .. 258-261(v.3-6), 263-265 (v.8-9); ch. 6 .. 461(v.42), 464-465(v.45)

birth and death, cycle of, ch. 2 .. 120(v.40), 124(v.43), 142(v.50); ch. 3 .. 234(v.35); ch. 4 .. 277(v.17), 311-312(v.37-38); ch. 5 .. 357-358(v.17); ch. 6 .. 398(v.6)

birth, bonds of, ch. 2 .. 143-145(v.51)

birth, divine (see also birth of Krishna), ch. 4 .. 265(v.9)

birth of Krishna, ch. 4 .. 258-265(v.4-9)

blessing of action, ch. 3 .. 193(v.8)

blessings of the gods, ch. 3 .. 194-195(v.9), 197(v.11), 199(v.12); ch. 4 .. 268(v.12), 293(v.25)

bliss, ch. 2 .. 118-119(v.40), 121(v.41), 161-163(v.60-61), 166 (v.66), 169(v.68); ch. 3 .. 190(v.7), 240(v.39); ch. 4 .. 264(v.8), 280(v.18), 285-286(v.20), 288(v.22), 299(v.31), 307(v.35); ch. 5 .. 341(v.7), 363(v.20), 365-366(v.21-22), 372(v.24); ch. 6 .. 424-425(v.20-21), 427(v.23), 433(v.25), 440(v.28), 443-444(v.30), 453(v.35), 455(v.36)

bliss and quality of bliss, difference between, ch. 6 .. 440(v.28)

bliss-consciousness (see also divine consciousness, transcendental consciousness), ch. 2 .. 89(v.10), 121(v.41), 136-137(v.48), 150(v.55), 154(v.56), 165-167(v.65-66), 170(v.70), 173 (v.72); ch. 3 .. 184(v.3), 186-187(v.3-4), 194(v.9), 198 (v.11), 201-202(v.13), 220(v.27), 223-224(v.28-29), 227-229(v.31-33), 233(v.35), 237(v.37); ch. 4 .. 266(v.10), 283 (v.19), 291(v.24), 298-300(v.29-31), 307(v.35), 311(v.38); ch. 5 .. 333(v.3), 362(v.20), 364-365(v.21), 368(v.22), 371-372(v.24), 374(v.25); ch. 6 .. 386(v.1), 399(v.7), 403 (v.10), 423-424(v.20), 430(v.24), 437(v.27)

body, ch. 1 .. 36-37(v.14); ch. 2 .. 92(v.13), 97-98(v.18), 99 (v.20), 100-101(v.22-23); ch. 3 .. 191-193(v.8), 195(v.9), 204(v.14), 221(v.27), 233-234(v.35), 243(v.43); ch. 4 .. 259(v.5), 264-265(v.8-9), 286-287(v.21), 292(v.24); ch. 5 ..

345-348(v.11), 357(v.17), 368-370(v.23), 372(v.24), 375 (v.26); ch. 6 .. 387(v.1), 402-405(v.10), 407-410(v.12-14), 412-413(v.15), 415(v.17), 417(v.17), 462(v.43), 464(v.45), 466(v.46)

body and mind, coordination of, ch. 1 .. 53(v.29); ch. 2 .. 123 (v.42); ch. 5 .. 340(v.7)

body and mind subdued, ch. 6 .. 402-405(v.10)

body, changing conditions of the, ch. 2 .. 92-93(v.13-14), 97 (v.18); ch. 4 .. 259(v.5)

body, dweller in the (see also *jiva*), ch. 2 .. 97-98(v.18), 103 (v.26); ch. 3 .. 240-241(v.40), 243(v.43); ch. 5 .. 350(v.13)

body, stilling the, ch. 6 .. 408(v.13)

bondage (see also binding influence of action), ch. 2 .. 95(v.15), 124(v.43), 142-145(v.50-51); ch. 3 .. 193-194(v.8-9), 197 (v.11), 213(v.20), 218(v.25), 221-223(v.27-28), 227(v.31), 229-230(v.33), 237(v.37), 238-239(v.38-39), 241(v.40), 244 (v.43); ch. 4 .. 250(intro.), 265(v.9), 271-275(v.14-16), 287(v.22), 291(v.24), 301(v.32), 305(v.34), 309(v.36); ch. 5 .. 333-334(v.3), 339-340(v.7), 348-349(v.12), 353-355(v.14-16), 357(v.17); ch. 6 .. 387(v.1), 395(v.5), 420 (v.18)

bondage, cause of, ch. 5 .. 354(v.15)

bondage, mechanics of, ch. 3 .. 239(v.39); ch. 5 .. 349(v.12)

bondage, natural seat of, ch. 3 .. 230-231(v.33-34)

bondage of action, freedom from, ch. 3 .. 187(v.4), 218(v.25)

bonds of birth, ch. 2 .. 143-145(v.51)

born (see also birth), ch. 2 .. 99(v.20); ch. 6 .. 461(v.41)

Brahma, ch. 3 .. 205-207(v.15); ch. 4 .. 253(v.1)

Brahma Vidya (wisdom of the Absolute), ch. 2 .. 75(intro.), 85 (v.7); ch. 3 .. 177(intro.)

Brahmabindu Upanishad, ch. 4 .. 299(v.30)

Brahman, ch. 2 .. 98(v.18), 172-174(v.72); ch. 3 .. 195(v.9); ch. 4 .. 262(v.7), 290-293(v.24-25), 299-300(v.31); ch. 5 .. 336-338(v.6), 344(v.10), 360-365(v.19-21), 371-372(v.24); ch. 6 .. 386(v.1), 437-442(v.27-29), 457(v.38)

Brahman, describing, ch. 6 .. 440-442(v.28-29)

Brahman, established in, ch. 5 .. 360-363(v.19-20)

Brahman, fixity in, ch. 4 .. 290-292(v.24)

Brahman, knower of, ch. 5 .. 361-363(v.20)

Brahman, manifestation of, ch. 4 .. 262(v.7)

Brahman, nature of, ch. 6 .. 440-442(v.28-29)

Brahman, path to, ch. 6 .. 457-458(v.38)

Brahman, Union with, ch. 5 .. 364-366(v.21)

Brahmananda (cosmic consciousness), ch. 4 .. 317(v.39); ch. 6 .. 428(v.23)

Brahmanirvana (freedom born of the state of *Brahma*), ch. 5 .. 372(v.24)

Brahmasutra, ch. 4 .. 256(v.2)

Brahmi-sthiti (cosmic consciousness), ch. 5 .. 365-367(v.21-22)

brahmin, ch. 1 .. 32(v.7); ch. 2 .. 132-133(v.46); ch. 5 .. 358-359(v.18)

bravery, ch. 1 .. 54(v.30), 71(v.46)

break away from tradition, ch. 4 .. 256(v.2)

breath, ch. 4 .. 295(v.27), 297-298(v.27-30); ch. 5 .. 357(v.17), 376-377(v.27); ch. 6 .. 408-409(v.13), 412-413(v.15)

breath, balanced, ch. 5 .. 376-377(v.27)

breath, control of the, ch. 5 .. 377(v.27)

breath, cosmic, ch. 6 .. 413(v.15)

breath, refinement of, ch. 4 .. 295(v.27), 298-299(v.29-30); ch. 6 .. 407(v.12)

breathing, ch. 2 .. 173(v.72); ch. 4 .. 298-299(v.30); ch. 6 .. 407(v.12)

breathing exercises, ch. 4 .. 297-298(v.29)

breathing, suspension of, ch. 4 .. 298(v.29); ch. 5 .. 377(v.27)

Brihadaranyaka Upanishad, ch. 2 .. 140(v.49)

burden in life, ch. 3 .. 191(v.8)

calming the senses, ch. 4 .. 294(v.26)

calmness, ch. 2 .. 166(v.66); ch. 5 .. 361(v.19); ch. 6 .. 389-393 (v.3), 411(v.14)

caste (see also social order), ch. 1 .. 65-68(v.41-43); ch. 5 .. 358-360(v.18)

caste *dharma,* ch. 2 .. 85(v.7)

castes, intermixture of, ch. 1 .. 66(v.41), 68(v.43)

catastrophe, ch. 1 .. 27(v.1), 44(v.23)

causation, ch. 2 .. 99(v.20)

cause, ch. 2 .. 127(v.45), 140(v.49)

cause and effect, ch. 2 .. 104(v.27), 123(v.42), 126-127(v.45), 140(v.49), 142(v.50); ch. 3 .. 205(v.15), 243-244(v.43); ch. 4 .. 311(v.37)

cause of action, ch. 2 .. 140(v.49)

cause of bondage, ch. 5 .. 354(v.15)

celibate, ch. 6 .. 410(v.14)

ceremonies, rites and rituals, ch. 1 .. 67(v.42); ch. 2 .. 123-124 (v.42-43), 132(v.46); ch. 3 .. 194-195(v.9), 198(v.11), 203-206(v.13-15); ch. 4 .. 268(v.12), 290(v.24), 297(v.28); ch. 6 .. 463(v.44), 466(v.46)

change, ch. 2 .. 92-93(v.12-14), 95-96(v.16), 97(v.18), 99-100 (v.20-21), 104-105(v.27); ch. 3 .. 233-234(v.35); ch. 5 .. 358(v.17), 368(v.22)

change, *dharma* of, ch. 3 .. 233-234(v.35)

changing conditions of the body, ch. 2 .. 92-93(v.13-14), 97(v.18); ch. 3 .. 234(v.35); ch. 4 .. 259(v.5)

channeled desire, ch. 3 .. 236(v.37)

channeling the mind in one direction (see also convergence, one-pointed), ch. 2 .. 121(v.41); ch. 6 .. 435-436(v.26), 452 (v.34)

characteristics of a realized man, ch. 2 .. 148-174(v.54-72); ch. 4 .. 278-292(v.18-24); ch. 5 .. 358-380(v.18-29); ch. 6 .. 397-401(v.6-9)

charm, increasing (see also natural tendency of the mind), ch. 2 .. 119(v.40), 121(v.41), 166(v.66), 169(v.68); ch. 4 .. 317 (v.39); ch. 5 .. 332(v.2); ch. 6 .. 403-404(v.10), 409-411 (v.14), 413(v.15), 436(v.26)

chastity, ch. 6 .. 409-410(v.14)

Chaturyugi (time span of four *yugas*), ch. 4 .. 254(v.1)

chitta (storehouse of impressions), ch. 6 .. 422(v.19)

civilization, highest, ch. 4 .. 254(v.1)

clarity, intellectual, ch. 1 .. 64(v.39)

coarse mind, ch. 3 .. 207(v.15)

coarseness in the nervous system, ch. 4 .. 309(v.36)

code of action, ch. 3 .. 186(v.3)

code of thinking, ch. 3 .. 186(v.3)

collect himself, ch. 6 .. 402-403(v.10), 412-414(v.15), 439-440 (v.28)

collision of desires, ch. 3 .. 236(v.37)

comfortable, ch. 6 .. 406(v.11)

command of nature, ch. 5 .. 360-361(v.19)

communication between heart and mind, ch. 1 .. 51(v.28)

communion of saints with God, ch. 6 .. 444(v.30)

communion with God, ch. 5 .. 380(v.29); ch. 6 .. 444(v.30)

compassion, ch. 1 .. 49(v.28); ch. 2 .. 76-78(v.1); ch. 5 .. 374 (v.25)

complete conception of *yagya*, ch. 3 .. 206(v.15)

complete success in life, ch. 3 .. 197(v.11)

concentration, ch. 2 .. 168(v.67); ch. 3 .. 229-231(v.33-34); ch. 5 .. 377(v.27); ch. 6 .. 408(v.13)

concern for others (see also living for others), ch. 1 .. 52(v.29), 56-57(v.32-33), 72(v.47); ch. 2 .. 83(v.1)

concrete, ch. 2 .. 92(v.12), 149(v.54); ch. 3 .. 213(v.20), 241 (v.40); ch. 4 .. 281(v.18), 304(v.34); ch. 5 .. 328(intro.)

conflicts, field of, ch. 2 .. 129(v.45), 137(v.48)

confusion, ch. 4 .. 320(v.41)

conquer the universe, ch. 5 .. 360-361(v.19)

conquered the senses, ch. 5 .. 338-341(v.7)

conscious mind (see also mind), ch. 2 .. 136(v.48); ch. 3 .. 236 (v.37); ch. 4 .. 282-284(v.19); ch. 6 .. 398(v.6), 422(v.19)

conscious thinking level (see also thinking level), ch. 3 .. 213-214(v.20)

consciousness, cosmic (see also *nitya-samadhi,* realization, separation of Self from activity), ch. 2 .. 132(v.46), 135-148(v.48-53), 150-174(v.55-72); ch. 3 .. 183-185(v.3), 187(v.4), 191-194(v.8-9), 201-202(v.13), 206(v.15), 208-213(v.17-20), 223(v.28), 225-226(v.30); ch. 4 .. 250-251(intro.), 266(v.10), 273(v.15), 276-277(v.17), 279-280(v.18), 283-285(v.19-20), 288-289(v.22-23), 291-293(v.24-25), 296-297 (v.27-28), 300-302(v.31-33), 305-307(v.35), 309(v.37), 313-318(v.38-39), 321(v.41-42); ch. 5 .. 326-327(intro.), 332-334(v.2-3), 336-348(v.5-11), 350-353(v.13-14), 356-358 (v.16-17), 360(v.19), 363-365(v.20-21), 367-370(v.22-23), 372(v.24), 375-376(v.26), 378(v.28); ch. 6 .. 385(v.1), 387(v.1), 389-394(v.2-4), 396-397(v.5), 402(v.10), 405 (v.10), 410-412(v.14), 418-420(v.17-18), 424-426(v.20-22), 428-431(v.23-24), 434(v.25), 436(v.26), 438-439(v.27-28), 444(v.30), 446-447(v.31), 451-455(v.33-36), 457-458 (v.38), 460(v.41), 464-465(v.45), 467-468(v.47)

consciousness, divine (see also bliss-consciousness), ch. 1 .. 45 (v.23); ch. 2 .. 172-174(v.71-72); ch. 3 .. 180(v.1), 190 (v.7), 206-207(v.15), 215(v.22), 241(v.41); ch. 4 .. 263 (v.8), 317(v.39); ch. 5 .. 329(intro.), 337(v.6), 339-341 (v.7), 345(v.10), 362(v.20), 371-375(v.24-26); ch. 6 .. 385 (v.1), 416(v.17), 428(v.23), 441(v.28), 443(v.30), 447 (v.31)

consciousness, dreaming state of, ch. 3 .. 184(v.3), 187-188(v.4-

5), 208(v.17); ch. 4 .. 314(v.38), 317(v.39); ch. 5 .. 338-340(v.7), 362(v.20)

consciousness, fourth state of (see also Self-consciousness, transcendental consciousness), ch. 3 .. 187(v.4)

consciousness, God-, ch. 3 .. 185(v.3), 187-188(v.4), 191-193(v.8), 196(v.9), 197-198(v.11), 200-202(v.12-13), 206-207(v.15-16), 209-213(v.18-20), 226-227(v.30-31), 240(v.39); ch. 4 .. 250-251(intro.), 264(v.8), 266-267(v.10-11), 271(v.14), 273(v.15), 276-277(v.17), 279-280(v.18), 283(v.19), 288 (v.22), 296-297(v.27-28), 300-302(v.31-33), 305-313(v.35-38), 315-318(v.38-39), 321(v.42); ch. 5 .. 327(intro.), 332 (v.2), 334(v.3), 336(v.5), 346-349(v.11-12), 353(v.14), 367(v.22), 379-380(v.29); ch. 6 .. 383(intro.), 391-394 (v.3-4), 396-397(v.5), 410-412(v.14), 414(v.15), 426(v.22), 428(v.23), 443-456(v.30-37), 458(v.38), 461(v.42), 464-467(v.45-47)

consciousness, God's, ch. 4 .. 268(v.11)

consciousness, level of (see also level of evolution), ch. 2 .. 107 (v.29), 155(v.56), 167(v.66); ch. 3 .. 186(v.3), 232(v.35); ch. 4 .. 276(v.17), 282-284(v.19), 288(v.22), 291(v.24), 299(v.31), 302(v.33), 314(v.38), 316(v.39); ch. 5 .. 367 (v.22), 380(v.29); ch. 6 .. 383(intro.), 396-397(v.5), 421 (v.19), 442-446(v.29-31), 449(v.32), 457-458(v.38), 460 (v.41)

consciousness, pure (see also transcendental consciousness), ch. 2 .. 129(v.45), 147-148(v.53), 152(v.55), 164(v.64); ch. 3 .. 190(v.7), 207(v.16), 214(v.20), 223(v.28), 228(v.32), 236(v.37), 238(v.38); ch. 4 .. 277(v.17), 291(v.24), 294-295(v.26-27), 302(v.33), 309-310(v.36-37), 312(v.38); ch. 5 .. 347(v.11), 361(v.19), 374(v.25); ch. 6 .. 394(v.4), 397(v.6), 407(v.12), 412(v.14), 418-419(v.17-18), 437 (v.27), 445(v.30)

consciousness, seat of, ch. 2 .. 173(v.72)

consciousness, sleep state of, ch. 1 .. 45(v.24); ch. 3 .. 184(v.3), 187-188(v.4-5), 208(v.17); ch. 4 .. 277(v.17), 314(v.38), 317(v.39); ch. 5 .. 338-340(v.7); ch. 6 .. 409(v.14), 413-416(v.15-17)

consciousness, transcendental (see also bliss-consciousness, pure consciousness, Self-consciousness), ch. 2 .. 121(v.41), 126 (v.45), 131(v.45), 135-137(v.48), 142(v.50), 144-148(v.51-53), 151(v.55), 153(v.55), 155(v.56), 158-159(v.58), 160 (v.59), 166-167(v.66), 173(v.72); ch. 3 .. 179(v.1), 183-186(v.3), 190(v.7), 194(v.9), 196(v.10), 198(v.11), 201-202(v.13), 212(v.19), 223(v.28), 225(v.30), 229(v.33); ch. 4 .. 266(v.10), 270(v.13), 282-283(v.19), 288-289(v.22-

23), 293(v.25), 296(v.27), 301-302(v.32-33), 306(v.35), 309(v.36), 312-314(v.38), 316-317(v.39), 321(v.42); ch. 5 .. 327-328(intro.), 332-334(v.2-3), 337(v.6), 346-348 (v.11), 357-358(v.17), 363-364(v.20-21), 369(v.23), 374 (v.25); ch. 6 .. 387-397(v.1-5), 405(v.10), 407(v.12), 410-412(v.14), 418-419(v.18), 423-425(v.20-21), 429-431(v.24), 433-436(v.25-26), 440(v.28), 452-453(v.34-35), 460(v.41), 463-466(v.44-46)

conciousness, vibrating, ch. 3 .. 236(v.37)

consciousness, waking state of, ch. 2 .. 173-174(v.72); ch. 3 .. 184(v.3), 186-188(v.3-5), 193-194(v.9), 201(v.13), 208 (v.17), 226(v.30); ch. 4 .. 277(v.17), 312-314(v.38), 316-317(v.39); ch. 5 .. 338-340(v.7), 362-364(v.20-21), 367 (v.22); ch. 6 .. 391(v.3), 415-416(v.16)

consummation of all action, ch. 4 .. 301(v.32)

contact of the self with the field of experience, ch. 5 .. 364-368 (v.21-22)

contact of the senses, ch. 2 .. 93-95(v.14-15); ch. 3 .. 236(v.37); ch. 4 .. 284(v.19); ch. 5   365-366(v.21-22), 376-377(v.27); ch. 6 .. 419(v.18)

contacting higher powers, ch. 3 .. 195(v.9); ch. 4 .. 268(v.12)

contemplation, ch. 3 .. 183-185(v.3); ch. 4 .. 322(v.42); ch. 6 .. 400(v.8)

content of action, ch. 3 .. 186(v.3)

content of thinking, ch. 3 .. 186(v.3)

contentment (see also peace), ch. 3 .. 201(v.13), 207-208(v.16-17), 211(v.19), 214-215(v.20-22), 218(v.25), 220(v.27), 225(v.30), 227(v.31); ch. 4 .. 266(v.10), 283-285(v.19-20), 288(v.22),294(v.26), 307(v.35), 318(v.39); ch. 5 .. 333 (v.3), 337(v.6), 361(v.19), 368(v.23), 371-372(v.24); ch. 6 .. 400-401(v.8-9), 409(v.14), 419-420(v.18), 423-424 (v.20), 455(v.36), 460(v.41), 467(v.47)

continuity of progress, ch. 3 .. 233(v.35)

contradiction, ch. 3 .. 181-183(v.1-2); ch. 4 .. 319(v.40); ch. 5 .. 327-329(intro.), 331(v.1); ch. 6 .. 385(v.1), 440(v.28)

contrast during transcendental meditation, ch. 6 .. 403(v.10)

contrast to Divinity, ch. 6 .. 426(v.22)

control (see also restraint), ch. 2 .. 156(v.57), 160-162(v.59-61), 164(v.64), 168-170(v.67-69); ch. 3 .. 229-231(v.33-34), 241-242(v.41); ch. 4 .. 293-296(v.26-27); ch. 5 .. 353(v.14), 360(v.19), 368(v.22), 375(v.26), 377-378(v.27-28); ch. 6 .. 403-405(v.10), 411(v.14), 429-432(v.24-25), 435(v.26), 451-452(v.34-35), 455(v.36)

control, difficulty of, ch. 4 .. 294(v.26); ch. 6 .. 451-452(v.34-35)

control of all levels of creation, ch. 5 .. 360(v.19)

control of the breath, ch. 5 .. 377(v.27)

control of the mind, ch. 4 .. 295(v.27); ch. 6 .. 452-453(v.35)

control of the senses, ch. 2 .. 160-162(v.59-61), 64(v.64); ch. 3 ..
    189-190(v.6-7), 244(v.43); ch. 4 .. 294-295(v.26-27); ch.
    5 .. 377(v.27); ch. 6 .. 429-431(v.24)

controlling thoughts, ch. 5 .. 375(v.26), 377(v.27)

convergence (see also one-pointed), ch. 2 .. 125-126(v.44-45),
    147-148(v.53), 166(v.66); ch. 3 .. 194(v.9); ch. 4 .. 294
    (v.26), 302(v.33); ch. 5 .. 371(v.24); ch. 6 .. 410(v.14),
    412(v.15)

cooking (see also food), ch. 3 .. 203(v.13)

coordination of all aspects of life, ch. 3 .. 195-196(v.9)

coordination of body and mind, ch. 1 .. 52-53(v.29); ch. 2 .. 123
    (v.42); ch. 5 .. 340(v.7)

coordination of heart and mind, ch. 1 .. 49-54(v.28-30)

coordination of mind and senses, ch. 2 .. 87(v.8); ch. 5 .. 340-
    341(v.7)

cosmic breath, ch. 6 .. 413(v.15)

cosmic consciousness (see also *nitya-samadhi,* realization, separa-
    tion of Self from activity), ch. 2 .. 132(v.46), 135-148(v.48-
    53), 150-174(v.55-72); ch. 3 .. 183-185(v.3), 187(v.4),
    191-194(v.8-9), 201-202(v.13), 206(v.15), 208-213(v.17-
    20), 223(v.28), 225-226(v.30); ch. 4 .. 250-251(intro.),
    266(v.10), 273(v.15), 276-277(v.17), 279-280(v.18), 283-
    285(v.19-20), 288-289(v.22-23), 291-293(v.24-25), 296-297
    (v.27-28), 300-302(v.31-33), 305-307(v.35), 309(v.37), 313-
    318(v.38-39), 321(v.41-42); ch. 5 .. 326-327(intro.), 332-
    334(v.2-3), 336-348(v.5-11), 350-353(v.13-14), 356-358
    (v.16-17), 360(v.19), 363-365(v.20-21), 367-370(v.22-23),
    372(v.24), 375-376(v.26), 378(v.28); ch. 6 .. 385(v.1),
    389-394(v.2-4), 396-397(v.5), 402(v.10), 405(v.10), 410-
    412(v.14), 418-420(v.17-18), 424-426(v.20-22), 428-431
    (v.23-24), 434(v.25), 436(v.26), 438-439(v.27-28), 444
    (v.30), 446-447(v.31), 451-455(v.33-36), 457-458(v.38),
    460(v.41), 464-465(v.45), 467-468(v.47)

cosmic consciousness, action in, ch. 3 .. 209-212(v.18-19), 217-
    227(v.24-30); ch. 4 .. 278-292(v.18-24)

cosmic consciousness, criterion of, ch. 5 .. 365(v.21)

cosmic consciousness, death in, ch. 3 .. 234(v.35); ch. 4 .. 291-
    292(v.24)

cosmic consciousness, desire in, ch. 2 .. 162(v.61); ch. 3 .. 237 (v.37)

cosmic consciousness, essential features of, ch. 6 .. 434(v.25)

cosmic consciousness, physiology of gaining, ch. 4 .. 314(v.38)

cosmic consciousness, resistance to development of, ch. 3 .. 191 (v.8)

cosmic consciousness, three prerequisites to, ch. 6 .. 438(v.27)

cosmic consciousness: transformation into God-consciousness, ch. 4 .. 307(v.35), 313(v.38), 315(v.38); ch. 5 .. 348(v.11)

cosmic ego, ch. 5 .. 343(v.8,9)

cosmic evolution, ch. 4 .. 289(v.23)

cosmic existence, ch. 2 .. 98(v.18); ch. 5 .. 341(v.7), 346(v.11); ch. 6 .. 419(v.18), 460(v.41), 468(v.47)

cosmic intelligence, ch. 2 .. 118(v.40), 137(v.48), 142(v.50), 165 (v.66), 172(v.71); ch. 4 .. 268(v.11), 304(v.34); ch. 5 .. 346-347(v.11), 365(v.21); ch. 6 .. 393(v.3), 397-398(v.6), 416(v.17)

cosmic law (see also laws of nature), ch. 1 .. 63-64(v.39); ch. 2 .. 133(v.46); ch. 5 .. 333(v.3)

cosmic life, ch. 1 .. 63(v.39); ch. 2 .. 98(v.18), 143(v.51); ch. 3 .. 187(v.4), 197(v.11), 202-203(v.13), 234(v.35); ch. 4 .. 250(intro.), 276(v.17), 279(v.18), 296(v.27), 315(v.38); ch. 5 .. 325(intro.), 346(v.11), 353(v.14); ch. 6 .. 392(v.3)

cosmic mind, ch. 2 .. 136-137(v.48); ch. 4 .. 304(v.34); ch. 6 .. 397(v.6), 464(v.45)

cosmic plan (see also divine plan), ch. 2 .. 172(v.71)

cosmic purpose, ch. 3 .. 192(v.8), 202-204(v.13-14), 209(v.18); ch. 4 .. 251(v.1), 276(v.17), 287(v.22); ch. 5 .. 346(v.11); ch. 6 .. 439(v.28)

cow, ch. 5 .. 358-359(v.18)

craving, ch. 2 .. 170-171(v.70); ch. 3 .. 239(v.39); ch. 6 .. 418-420(v.18)

creation, ch. 2 .. 128-129(v.45); ch. 3 .. 188(v.5), 196-198(v.10-11), 200(v.12), 201(v.13), 216(v.23), 225(v.30); ch. 4 .. 252(v.1), 254(v.1), 261-262(v.6-7), 269-272(v.13-14), 276 (v.17), 284(v.19), 296(v.27), 309(v.36); ch. 5 .. 325(intro.), 340(v.7), 346(v.11), 352(v.14), 359-360(v.18-19), 375 (v.26), 380(v.29); ch. 6 .. 392(v.3), 424-425(v.21), 427 (v.23), 442(v.29), 444-446(v.30-31), 448-449(v.32), 461 (v.41), 467(v.47)

creation and evolution, purpose of, ch. 1 .. 62(v.37); ch. 2 .. 104 (v.27); ch. 3 .. 204(v.14), 236-237(v.37); ch. 5 .. 352(v.14), 380(v.29)

creation, author of, ch. 4 .. 270(v.13)

creation, first manifestation of, ch. 3 .. 206(v.15)

creation, Lord of, ch. 2 .. 162(v.61); ch. 3 .. 196(v.10), 216(v.22), 225-226(v.30), 228(v.32); ch. 6 .. 411(v.14), 414(v.15), 446(v.31)

creation, process of, ch. 3 .. 206(v.15)

creation, second manifestation of, ch. 3 .. 206(v.15)

creation, source of, ch. 3 .. 206-207(v.15-16); ch. 4 .. 270-271 (v.13-14)

creation, subtlest level of, ch. 2 .. 169(v.68); ch. 3 .. 222(v.28)

creation, supreme level of, ch. 6 .. 446(v.31)

creation, wheel of, ch. 3 .. 208(v.16)

creative intelligence, ch. 1 .. 66(v.41)

Creator (see also *Brahma,* God), ch. 3 .. 196(v.10), 206(v.15), 225-226(v.30); ch. 4 .. 253(v.1), 270(v.13)

Creator, intimacy with the, ch. 3 .. 225-226(v.30)

criteria of a *sanyasi,* ch. 5 .. 333-334(v.3); ch. 6 .. 384-389(v.1-2)

criteria of a *yogi,* ch. 2 .. 148-174(v.54-72); ch. 6 .. 384-389(v.1-2)

criterion of being united with the Divine, ch. 5 .. 370(v.23)

criterion of cosmic consciousness, ch. 5 .. 365(v.21)

criterion of natural duty, ch. 3 .. 192(v.8)

criterion of vision in enlightenment, ch. 5 .. 358-360(v.18)

culture of both mental and physical aspects, ch. 5 .. 369(v.23)

culture of the nervous system, ch. 4 .. 314-315(v.38); ch. 6 .. 431(v.24)

custodians of Vedic wisdom, ch. 4 .. 256(v.2)

cycle of action, impression and desire, ch. 2 .. 142(v.50); ch. 4 .. 284-286(v.19-20)

cycle of birth and death, ch. 2 .. 120(v.40), 124(v.43), 142(v.50); ch. 3 .. 234(v.35); ch. 4 .. 277(v.17), 311-312(v.37-38); ch. 5 .. 357-358(v.17); ch. 6 .. 398(v.6)

cycle of cause and effect, ch. 2 .. 142(v.50); ch. 4 .. 311(v.37)

daily life, routine of, ch. 6 .. 415-416(v.16-17), 453(v.35)

danger, ch. 3 .. 232-233(v.35); ch. 4 .. 257(v.2), 263(v.7), 288 (v.22)

danger, greatest, ch. 3 .. 233(v.35)

death, ch. 2 .. 92-94(v.13-15), 97(v.18), 99(v.20), 103-104(v.26-27), 107(v.30); ch. 3 .. 231-234(v.35); ch. 4 .. 265(v.9), 291-292(v.24); ch. 5 .. 375-376(v.26); ch. 6 .. 460-462 (v.41-43)

death, after, ch. 5 .. 375-376(v.26)

death in cosmic consciousness, ch. 3 .. 234(v.35); ch. 4 .. 291-292(v.24)

decadence in modern society (see also social disorder), ch. 2 .. 152-153(v.55)

decadence, spiritual, ch. 4 .. 257(v.2)

decay of *dharma,* ch. 4 .. 262-263(v.7)

deep sleep, inactivity of, ch. 3 .. 187(v.4)

deep sleep state, ch. 1 .. 45(v.24); ch. 3 .. 184(v.3), 187-188(v.4-5), 208(v.17); ch. 4 .. 277(v.17), 314(v.38), 317(v.39); ch. 5 .. 338-340(v.7); ch. 6 .. 409(v.14), 413-416(v.15-17)

definition of *Yoga,* ch. 6 .. 422-428(v.19-23)

degree of happiness, ch. 2 .. 119(v.40); ch. 5 .. 367(v.22); ch. 6 .. 461(v.41)

delusion, ch. 2 .. 146(v.52), 163-164(v.62-63); ch. 3 .. 189(v.6), 220-221(v.27), 224-225(v.29-30), 228(v.32), 240-241(v.40); ch. 4 .. 305-306(v.35), 309(v.36), 318(v.39); ch. 5 .. 354(v.15), 361-363(v.20); ch. 6 .. 386(v.1), 441(v.28), 457-458(v.38)

describing *Brahman,* ch. 6 .. 440-442(v.28-29)

desire, ch. 1 .. 51(v.28), 56-57(v.32), 58(v.34); ch. 2 .. 124(v.43), 134(v.47), 140(v.49), 142(v.50), 150-154(v.55), 158-159(v.58), 162-164(v.61-64), 170-172(v.70-71); ch. 3 .. 196(v.10), 199-200(v.12), 208-209(v.17-18), 218(v.25), 220(v.27), df. 236(v.37), 236-245(v.37-43); ch. 4 .. 268(v.12), 280-286(v.18-21); ch. 5 .. 333-334(v.3), 348-349(v.12), 368-370(v.23), 374-376(v.26), 377-378(v.28); ch. 6 .. 387-389(v.1-2), 393-394(v.4), 427(v.23), 429-430(v.24), 437(v.27), 455(v.36)

desire, abandoning, ch. 3 .. 242(v.41); ch. 5 .. 370(v.23); ch. 6 .. 429-430(v.24)

desire, absence of, ch. 1 .. 51(v.28)

desire, abstract and concrete, ch. 3 .. 241(v.40)

desire, binding influence of (see also bondage), ch. 3 .. 239(v.39)

desire, channeled, ch. 3 .. 236(v.37)

desire, flow of, ch. 1 .. 51(v.28), 56(v.32); ch. 3 .. 236(v.37), 239(v.39), 242(v.41)

desire, formation of, ch. 4 .. 284(v.19)

desire, fountainhead of, ch. 3 .. 242(v.41)

desire, fulfilment of, ch. 2 .. 162-163(v.61-62); ch. 3 .. 196(v.10), 241(v.40), 245(v.43); ch. 4 .. 280(v.18)

desire in cosmic consciousness, ch. 2 .. 162(v.61); ch. 3 .. 237 (v.37)

desire in the state of ignorance, ch. 3 .. 237(v.37)

desire, incentive of, ch. 4 .. 284-285(v.19); ch. 6 .. 388-389(v.2), 393-394(v.4)

desire, influence of, ch. 3 .. 239(v.39)

desire, insatiable, ch. 3 .. 238-240(v.39)

desire, machinery that gives rise to, ch. 3 .. 240-241(v.39-40)

desire, obstruction of, ch. 3 .. 236-237(v.37)

desire of the master, ch. 4 .. 304(v.34)

desire of the righteous, ch. 4 .. 264(v.8)

desire, resistance of, ch. 1 .. 56(v.32)

desire, seat of, ch. 3 .. 240-242(v.40-41)

desire, seed of, ch. 2 .. 142(v.50), 158(v.58); ch. 5 .. 341(v.7); ch. 6 .. 388-389(v.2), 394(v.4), 422(v.19)

desire, source of, ch. 3 .. 238(v.38)

desireless action, ch. 3 .. 209(v.18)

desirelessness, ch. 6 .. 387(v.1)

desires and mind, ch. 3 .. 243(v.43)

desires, collision of, ch. 3 .. 236(v.37)

desires, free from, ch. 2 .. 152(v.55); ch. 4 .. 281-284(v.19), 286-287(v.21-22); ch. 5 .. 333(v.3), 374-376(v.26), 377-378 (v.28)

desires, goal of all, ch. 2 .. 170(v.70)

desires, identified with, ch. 2 .. 151(v.55)

desires, inability to fulfill, ch. 2 .. 163(v.62)

desires of the mind, ch. 2 .. 151(v.55)

desires on the surface, ch. 2 .. 151(v.55)

desires, purpose of all, ch. 2 .. 170(v.70); ch. 3 .. 208-209(v.17-18)

desires, subduing, ch. 3 .. 243-254(v.43)

desires, worldly, ch. 2 .. 151(v.55)

destroyer of knowledge and realization, ch. 3 .. 241-242(v.41)

destruction, ch. 1 .. 38(v.15), 41(v.19), 44(v.23), 54(v.30), 66 (v.41); ch. 3 .. 217(v.24), 236-237(v.37); ch. 4 .. 263-264 (v.8), 269(v.13); ch. 6 .. 459(v.40)

destruction of ignorance, ch. 5 .. 355(v.16)

destruction of intellect, ch. 2 .. 163-164(v.63)

destruction of social order, ch. 1 .. 66-67(v.42), 70(v.45)

detachment (see also non-attachment, separation of Self from activity), ch. 1 .. 58(v.34); ch. 2 .. 156-157(v.57); ch. 3 ..

208(v.17), 210(v.19), 244(v.43), 306(v.35); ch. 5 .. 332 (v.2), 349(v.12), 380(v.29); ch. 6 .. 396(v.5)

detachment, perfect, ch. 5 .. 334(v.3)

development, basic principle of, ch. 6 .. 395(v.5)

development, spiritual, ch. 3 .. 185(v.3); ch. 4 .. 255(v.2), 318 (v.40)

devotee, ch. 2 .. 86(v.7), 131(v.45); ch. 4 .. 258(v.3), 264(v.8); ch. 6 .. 445-450(v.30-33), 468(v.47)

devotee and God, difference between, ch. 6 .. 448(v.32)

devotion, ch. 2 .. 85-86(v.7), 131(v.45), 161-163(v.61); ch. 3 .. 193(v.8), 211(v.19), 227(v.31); ch. 4 .. 288(v.22), 306-307(v.35), 313(v.38), 315(v.18), 318(v.39); ch. 5 .. 332 (v.2), 348(v.11), 356-357(v.17), 373(v.25); ch. 6 .. 446-447(v.31-32), 453(v.35), 467-468(v.47)

dharma, ch. 1 .. df. 26-27(v.1), 26-29(v.1), 43(v.21), 54(v.30), 64-70(v.39-45); ch. 2 .. 84-86(v.7), 108-110(v.31-33), 115 (v.38), 117-120(v.40), 127(v.45), 130(v.45); ch. 3 .. 179-181(v.1), 191-192(v.8), 231-234(v.35); ch. 4 .. 262-264 (v.7-8), df. 262(v.7), 276-277(v.17), 288(v.22); ch. 6 .. 390(v.3), 417(v.17), df. 427(v.23), 456(v.37)

dharma, decay of, ch. 4 .. 262-263(v.7)

dharma, eternal, ch. 3 .. 233-234(v.35)

dharma, family, ch. 1 .. 64-70(v.40-45); ch. 2 .. 84-85(v.7)

dharma, fulfilment of, ch. 6 .. 427(v.23)

dharma, individual, ch. 1 .. 70(v.45)

dharma, merit of, ch. 3 .. 232(v.35)

dharma of another, ch. 3 .. 231-234(v.35)

dharma of continuous change, ch. 3 .. 233-234(v.35)

dharma of the Self, ch. 3 .. 233-235(v.35-36)

dharma of the three gunas, ch. 3 .. 233-234(v.35)

Dhyana Yoga (the Yoga of Meditation), ch. 6 .. 468(v.47)

die for others, ch. 2 .. 111(v.34)

difference between bliss and quality of bliss, ch. 6 .. 440(v.28)

difference between man and God, ch. 4 .. 259(v.5)

difference between the devotee and God, ch. 6 .. 448(v.32)

different schools of thought, ch. 2 .. 147(v.53); ch. 6 .. 450(v.32)

difficulty of control, ch. 4 .. 294(v.26); ch. 6 .. 451-452(v.34-35)

dignity, ch. 3 .. 202-203(v.13)

direct experience (see also experience, knowledge and experience), ch. 2 .. 106(v.29), 116-121(v.39-41), 128-129(v.45), 137 (v.48), 146-148(v.52-53), 152(v.55); ch. 3 .. 177(intro.),

187(v.4), 214(v.20), 222-223(v.28); ch. 4 .. 249(intro.), 280(v.18), 305(v.34), 319-320(v.40-41); ch. 5 .. 334(v.4), 355-356(v.16), 363(v.20); ch. 6 .. 400(v.8), 466(v.46)

direction of activity, ch. 4 .. 268(v.12)

direction of the senses, ch. 4 .. 295-296(v.27)

discipline, ch. 5 .. 374-376(v.26); ch. 6 .. 435(v.26), 454-455 (v.36)

disciplined action, ch. 2 .. 122(v.42)

disciplined mind, ch. 6 .. 412-413(v.15), 439(v.28), 454-455(v.36)

disciplined thoughts, ch. 2 .. 122-123 (v.42); ch. 5 .. 374-376(v.26)

discomfort during transcendental meditation, ch. 6 .. 432(v.25)

discourse, skill of the, ch. 3 .. 215(v.21), 266(v.30); ch. 4 .. 278 (v.17), 302(v.33); ch. 5 .. 327-328(intro.); ch. 6 .. 426 (v.22), 442(v.29)

discourses of enlightened men, ch. 6 .. 421(v.19)

discrimination (see also intellect), ch. 2 .. 152(v.55); ch. 3 .. 183-185(v.3), 230(v.33); ch. 4 .. 304(v.34); ch. 5 .. 348(v.11); ch. 6 .. 400(v.8), 433(v.25)

discrimination, impartial, ch. 3 .. 185(v.3)

discrimination in the process of meditation, ch. 6 .. 433(v.25)

disgrace, ch. 2 .. 110-111(v.34)

disinterestedness, ch. 3 .. 209(v.18)

disorder, family, ch. 1 .. 69(v.44)

disorder, social, ch. 1 .. 66-67(v.42), 70(v.45); ch. 4 .. 262-263 (v.7)

dispassionate, ch. 2 .. 156(v.57)

dissolution, ch. 5 .. 352(v.14)

distraction during transcendental meditation, ch. 6 .. 436(v.26)

disturbance during meditation, ch. 6 .. 403(v.10)

disunion, ch. 6 .. 426-427(v.23)

diversity (see also multiplicity), ch. 2 .. 125(v.44), 137(v.48), 161(v.60); ch. 3 .. 177(intro.); ch. 4 .. 256(v.2), 276 (v.17), 290(v.24), 307(v.35), 316(v.38); ch. 5 .. 340(v.7), 358-359(v.18); ch. 6 .. 400(v.8), 409(v.14), 442(v.29), 448-449(v.32)

dividing the mind, ch. 3 .. 185(v.3), 218-219(v.26)

Divine (see also Supreme), ch. 2 .. 134-135(v.47), 163(v.62); ch. 3 .. 185(v.3), 198(v.11), 206(v.15), 215(v.22), 218-219 (v.25-26), 228(v.32); ch. 4 .. 263(v.8), 265(v.9), 303(v.33), 317(v.39); ch. 5 .. 325(intro.), 329(intro.), 332(v.2), 342

(v.8,9), 344-346(v.8-11), 348-349(v.12), 362(v.20), 368-373(v.23-25), 375(v.26); ch. 6 .. 388(v.2), 391-393(v.3-4), 420(v.18), 445(v.30), 448(v.32)

divine activity, ch. 3 .. 216(v.22); ch. 4 .. 264-265(v.19)

divine birth (see also birth of Krishna), ch. 4 .. 265(v.9)

divine consciousness (see also bliss-consciousness), ch. 1 .. 45 (v.23); ch. 2 .. 172-174(v.71-72); ch. 3 .. 180(v.1), 190 (v.7), 206-207(v.15), 215(v.22), 241(v.41); ch. 4 .. 263 (v.8), 317(v.39); ch. 5 .. 329(intro.), 337(v.6), 339-341 (v.7), 345(v.10), 362(v.20), 371-375(v.24-26); ch. 6 .. 385 (v.1), 416(v.17), 428(v.23), 441(v.28), 443(v.30), 447(v.31)

Divine, drama of the, ch. 5 .. 373(v.25)

divine Incarnation, ch. 4 .. 259-265(v.5-9)

Divine, instrument of the, ch. 4 .. 287(v.22); ch. 5 .. 346(v.11)

Divine, knowledge of the, ch. 4 .. 308(v.36); ch. 5 .. 354(v.15)

divine manifestation, ch. 4 .. 261-262(v.6-7)

Divine Mother, ch. 4 .. 253(v.1)

divine plan (see also cosmic plan), ch. 3 .. 209(v.18), 218(v.25)

divine play, experience of the, ch. 6 .. 416(v.17)

Divine, playground for the, ch. 4 .. 250(intro.), 260(v.5)

divine revelation, ch. 4 .. 264(v.8)

divine will, ch. 5 .. 346(v.11)

Divinity, contrast to, ch. 6 .. 426(v.22)

Divinity, state of, ch. 4 .. 265(v.9), 267(v.11)

division of society (see also caste), ch. 3 .. 191-192(v.8)

doer (see also actor), ch. 2 .. 98(v.18-19), 134(v.47), 142-143 (v.50); ch. 3 .. 187(v.4), 191-192(v.8), 194(v.9), 197(v.11), 218(v.25), 220-221(v.27); ch. 4 .. 276-277(v.17), 283 (v.19), 310(v.37); ch. 5 .. 325(intro.), 350-353(v.13-14)

doer, action and its fruits (link between), ch. 5 .. 351-353(v.14)

doer and his work, ch. 3 .. 191(v.8)

dog, ch. 5 .. 358-359(v.18)

doomed, ch. 3 .. 228(v.32)

doubt, ch. 2 .. 146(v.52); ch. 3 .. 227(v.31); ch. 4 .. 317-322 (v.39-42); ch. 5 .. 326(intro.), 346(v.11), 373-374(v.25); ch. 6 .. 450(v.33), 457-458(v.38-39)

doubting mind, ch. 4 .. 318-319(v.40)

drama of the Divine, ch. 5 .. 373(v.25)

dreaming state, ch. 3 .. 184(v.3), 187-188(v.4-5), 208(v.17); ch. 4 .. 314(v.38), 317(v.39); ch. 5 .. 338-340(v.7), 362(v.20)

duality, ch. 1 .. 49-53(v.28); ch. 2 .. 126-132(v.45); ch. 3 .. 211
      (v.19); ch. 4 .. 250(intro.), 288(v.22), 291(v.24), 305-306
      (v.35), 315(v.38); ch. 5 .. 347(v.11); ch. 6 .. 391(v.3),
      394(v.4), 409-410(v.14), 426(v.22), 468(v.47)

dullness, ch. 2 .. 156(v.57), 171(v.70); ch. 3 .. 239(v.39); ch. 6 ..
      406(v.12), 415(v.16), 433(v.25), 454(v.36)

duty, ch. 1 .. 49-50(v.28), 53-54(v.30), 60-61(v.36), 71(v.47);
      ch. 2 .. 76(v.1), 97(v.17), 107-108(v.30-31), 113(v.37);
      ch. 3 .. 191-193(v.8), 195(v.9), 216(v.23), 219(v.26), 322
      (v.42); ch. 6 .. 386(v.1), 466(v.46)

duty, allotted (see also *dharma*), ch. 3 .. 191-193(v.8)

duty, natural, ch. 2 .. 108(v.31), 113(v.37); ch. 3 .. 191-193(v.8)

Dvapara-Yuga, ch. 4 .. 254(v.1)

dvitiyad vai bhayam bhavati (certainly fear is born of duality),
      ch. 1 .. 50(v.28)

dweller in the body, ch. 2 .. 97-98(v.18), 103(v.26); ch. 3 .. 240-
      241(v.40), 243(v.43); ch. 5 .. 350(v.13)

dynamic nature, ch. 6 .. 454(v.36)

earning of food, ch. 3 .. 203(v.13)

earth, life on, ch. 5 .. 358(v.17); ch. 6 .. 461(v.41)

easy (see also automatic, effortless, simplicity of transcendental
      meditation), ch. 2 .. 136(v.48), 143(v.50); ch. 3 .. 186
      (v.3), 229(v.33), 239(v.39), 244(v.43); ch. 4 .. 294(v.26);
      ch. 5 .. 332-334(v.2-3), 337(v.6), 370(v.23); ch. 6 .. 413
      (v.15), 428(v.23), 435(v.26), 439-441(v.28), 451(v.34),
      453(v.35), 455(v.36), 464(v.45), 466(v.46)

eat, ch. 6 .. 414-415(v.16)

eat the remains of *yagya,* ch. 3 .. 200-203(v.13); ch. 4 .. 299(v.31)

education, ch. 1 .. 45(v.23)

effort, ch.2 .. 117-120(v.40); ch. 4 .. 268(v.12); ch. 5 .. 377
      (v.27); ch. 6 .. 417(v.17), 456(v.37), 463(v.44), 465-466
      (v.45-46)

effortless (see also automatic, easy, simplicity of transcendental
      meditation), ch. 2 .. 117-20(v.40), 143-145(v.50-51); ch.
      3 .. 210(v.19); ch. 5 .. 377(v.27); ch. 6 .. 417(v.17)

ego, ch. 2 .. 98(v.18), 171-172(v.71); ch. 3 .. 204(v.14), 221
      (v.27), 223(v.28); ch. 5 .. 339(v.7), 372(v.24)

ego, cosmic, ch. 5 .. 343(v.8,9)

ego, functioning of the, ch. 3 .. 206(v.15)

ego, individual, ch. 2 .. 172(v.71); ch. 3 .. 206(v.15), 221(v.27);
      ch. 5 .. 343(v.8,9)

egocentricity, ch. 5 .. 374(v.25)

elements, five, ch. 6 .. 424-425(v.21)

elephant, ch. 5 .. 358-360(v.18)

emotions (see also feeling), ch. 4 .. 293(v.25), 315(v.38); ch. 6 .. 444(v.30)

endeavor, man of, ch. 6 .. 454(v.36)

endurance, ch. 6 .. 450(v.33)

enemy, ch. 3 .. 230-231(v.34), 236-240(v.37-39), 243-245(v.43); ch. 6 .. 395-399(v.5-6)

enemy, his own, ch. 6 .. 395-399(v.5-6)

energy, ch. 2 .. 105(v.28), 134(v.47), 141(v.49); ch. 3 .. 196 (v.10), 206(v.15), 236(v.37); ch. 4 .. 270(v.13), 300(v.31); ch. 5 .. 335(v.5), 361(v.19), 374(v.25); ch. 6 .. 410(v.14), 415(v.16), 417(v.17)

energy directed upward, ch. 6 .. 410(v.14)

enjoyer, ch. 2 .. 98(v.18)

enjoyer of *yagyas* and austerities, ch. 5 .. 379(v.29)

enjoyment (see also appreciation, happiness), ch. 2 .. 124-125 (v.44), 167-169(v.67-68); ch. 3 .. 199-200(v.12); ch. 5 .. 367(v.22); ch. 6 .. 415(v.16)

enlightened man (see also realized man, integrated man), ch. 3 .. 224(v.29), 229-230(v.33); ch. 4 .. 291(v.24), 304(v.34)

enlightened man, action of (see also characteristics of realized man), ch. 4 .. 281-292(v.19-24)

enlightened man distinguished from God, ch. 3 .. 215-216(v.22)

enlightened men, discourses of, ch. 6 .. 421(v.19)

enlightenment (see also fulfilment, realization), ch. 2 .. 132-133 (v.46), 144(v.51), 169-170(v.69); ch. 3 .. 186(v.3), 213 v.20), 215(v.22), 219(v.26), 229-230(v.33), 244(v.43); ch. 4 .. 249(intro.), 291(v.24), 295-296(v.27), 301-305 (v.32-34), 308-309(v.36), 317-321(v.39-42); ch. 5 .. 326 (intro.), 340(v.7), 343-344(v.8,9), 354(v.15), 373-374 (v.24-25); ch. 6 .. 387(v.1), 447(v.32), 466(v.46)

enlightenment, action in (see also action in cosmic consciousness), ch. 3 .. 217-218(v.25)

enlightenment, how to gain, ch. 4 .. 303-305(v.34)

envy, ch. 4 .. 287-288(v.22)

equanimity, ch. 2 .. 94(v.15), 113-115(v.38), 135(v.48), 139 (v.49), 154(v.56), 156(v.57); ch. 5 .. 360-361(v.19); ch. 6 .. 384(intro.), 455(v.36)

equanimity, basis of, ch. 5 .. 361(v.19)

equilibrium (see also balancing force of nature), ch. 1 .. 27(v.1), 64-65(v.40); ch. 4 .. 262(v.7), 264(v.8), 269(v.13), 288 (v.22)

essence of *Sankhya,* ch. 2 .. 91-95(v.12-15), 117(v.39)

essence of *Yoga,* ch. 2 .. 126-138(v.45-48)

essential constituent of manifest creation, ch. 3 .. 220(v.27)

essential feature of life, ch. 5 .. 369(v.23)

essential features of cosmic consciousness, ch. 6 .. 434(v.25)

essential nature of mind, ch. 2 .. 78(v.2)

essential wisdom of the *Bhagavad-Gita,* ch. 2 .. 117(v.39)

essentials of steady intellect, ch. 2 .. 150-161(v.55-59)

established in *Brahman,* ch. 5 .. 360-363(v.19-20)

established in *Yoga,* ch. 2 .. 135-138(v.48); ch. 6 .. 441-443(v.29)

established intellect (see also balanced intellect, steady intellect), ch. 2 .. 155-162(v.55-61), 165-167(v.66), 168-171(v.68-70); ch. 3 .. 180(v.1), 206(v.15), 209(v.18); ch. 5 .. 361(v.19)

eternal *dharma,* ch. 3 .. 233-234(v.35)

eternal freedom (see also freedom, liberation), ch. 2 .. 95(v.15), 117(v.39), 118(v.40), 142(v.50), 145(v.51), 172-174(v.72); ch. 3 .. 179(v.1), 186(v.3), 193(v.8), 198(v.11), 202-203 (v.13), 234(v.35), 237(v.37), 239(v.39), 245(v.43); ch. 4 .. 250(intro.), 272(v.14), 275(v.16), 280(v.18), 302(v.33), 311(v.37), 320(v.41); ch. 5 .. 325(intro.), 329(intro.), 332-333(v.2-3), 338(v.6), 340-341(v.7), 346(v.11), 353-354 (v.14-15), 357(v.17), 371-375(v.24-26); ch. 6 .. 411(v.14), 420(v.18), 441(v.28), 448(v.32)

eternal happiness, ch. 5 .. 364-368(v.21-22); ch. 6 .. 441(v.28)

eternal life, ch. 2 .. 92(v.12-13), 94-95(v.15), 99(v.20), 144-145 (v.51), 163(v.61); ch. 3 .. 195(v.9), 200(v.12), 205(v.15), 226(v.30); ch. 4 .. 253(v.1), 265(v.9); ch. 6 .. 392-393 (v.3), 425(v.21), 445(v.30), 449(v.32), 460(v.41)

eternal playground for the Divine, ch. 4 .. 250(intro.), 260(v.5)

eternity, ch. 4 .. 253(v.1)

evening meditation (see also meditation, transcendental meditation), ch. 4 .. 313(v.38); ch. 5 .. 344(v.10), 357(v.17)

evenness of mind (see also balance of mind), ch. 2 .. 94-95(v.15), 121(v.41), 164(v.64); ch. 4 .. 288(v.22); ch. 5 .. 361(v.19); ch. 6 .. 401(v.9), 451(v.34)

evenness of vision, ch. 5 .. 359-360(v.18); ch. 6 .. 420(v.18), 441-442(v.29), 447-448(v.32), 450(v.33)

events, value of, ch. 4 .. 252(v.1)

evil, ch. 1 .. 41(v.19); ch. 2 .. 127(v.45); ch. 3 .. 236-237(v.37), 241-242(v.41); ch. 4 .. 263-264(v.7-8), 274-275(v.16), 308-309(v.36)

evolution, ch. 1 .. 51(v.28), 64-65(v.40), 66(v.41), 68-69(v.44); ch. 2 .. 104(v.27), 108-109(v.31-33), 111(v.34), 113(v.37), 118(v.40), 122(v.42), 128(v.45), 130(v.45), 134(v.47), 143(v.51), 147(v.53), 155(v.56), 160(v.59), 167(v.66); ch. 3 .. 179(v.1), 191-192(v.8), 194-198(v.9-11), 201-204 (v.13-14), 206-207(v.15-16), 215-216(v.21-23), 219(v.26), 231-234(v.35); ch. 4 .. 262-264(v.7-8), 268-269(v.12-13), 273(v.15), 276-277(v.17), 280(v.18), 284(v.19), 288(v.22), 290-291(v.23-24), 293(v.25), 296-297(v.27-28), 300(v.32), 302-303(v.33), 309(v.36), 318(v.39); ch. 5 .. 325(intro.), 346(v.11), 352(v.14), 358(v.17), 375(v.26); ch. 6 .. 383 (intro.), 449(v.32)

evolution, cosmic, ch. 4 .. 289(v.23)

evolution, highest state of, ch. 3 .. 196(v.10); ch. 6 .. 467-468 (v.47)

evolution, laws of, ch. 1 .. 68(v.43); ch. 4 .. 273(v.15)

evolution, level of (see also level of consciousness, stages of evolution), ch. 3 .. 195(v.9), 232-234(v.35); ch. 4 .. 276(v.17); ch. 5 .. 352(v.14); ch. 6 .. 396(v.5), 410(v.14), 448(v.32)

evolution, mechanics of, ch. 1 .. 27(v.1)

evolution, process of, ch. 3 .. 188(v.5), 231(v.35), 233(v.35)

evolution, purpose of, ch. 4 .. 291(v.24)

evolution, retarding, ch. 3 .. 233(v.35)

evolution, stages of (see also level of consciousness, level of evolution), ch. 3 .. 193(v.8), 231-232(v.35), 234(v.35)

example, ch. 3 .. 214-217(v.21-24), 219(v.26)

excess, ch. 6 .. 415-418(v.16-17)

excitement, ch. 5 .. 368-370(v.23), 375(v.26)

exercises, breathing, ch. 4 .. 297-298(v.29)

exertion (see also control), ch. 6 .. 432(v.25)

existence, ch. 3 .. 188(v.5), 222-223(v.28); ch. 5 .. 357(v.17); ch. 6 .. 464(v.45)

existence, planes of, ch. 6 .. 460-461(v.41)

expansion of happiness, ch. 1 .. 62(v.37); ch. 3 .. 236(v.37); ch. 5 .. 352(v.14), 380(v.29); ch. 6 .. 415(v.16)

expectation, ch. 4 .. 286(v.21); ch. 6 .. 403-404(v.10)

experience (see also direct experience, knowledge and experience), ch. 2 .. 93(v.14), 116-117(v.39), 146-148(v.52-53), 155-156(v.57), 158(v.58), 165-169(v.65-68); ch. 3 .. 177-178

(intro.), 183(v.3), 194(v.9), 203(v.13), 206(v.15), 210-211 (v.19), 213(v.20), 219(v.26), 221(v.27), 223-226(v.28-30), 231(v.34); ch. 4 .. 249-250(intro.), 271-272(v.14), 283-286 (v.19-20), 294-295(v.26-27), 307(v.35), 316-317(v.39), 320(v.41), 322(v.42); ch. 5 .. 326(intro.), 330(v.1), 334 (v.4), 336-339(v.5-7), 341-343(v.7-9), 358(v.18), 362-368 (v.20-22), 372(v.24); ch. 6 .. 385(v.1), 387(v.1), 389-390 (v.2-3), 394(v.4), 396(v.5), 398(v.6), 402-405(v.10), 406-407(v.12), 420-425(v.18-21), 432-434(v.25), 437-439(v.27-28), 443-444(v.30), 468(v.47)

experience, faculty of, ch. 6 .. 437(v.27)

experience in God-consciousness, ch. 4 .. 307-308(v.35), 316 (v.38); ch. 6 .. 448(v.32)

experience, lack of, ch. 6 .. 464(v.45)

experience, mystical, ch. 6 .. 444-445(v.30)

experience, object of, ch. 3 .. 230-231(v.33-34); ch. 5 .. 343-344 (v.8,9); ch. 6 .. 421-422(v.19), 468(v.47)

experience, objective, ch. 6 .. 398(v.6), 421(v.19)

experience of happiness, ch. 2 .. 121(v.41), 166(v.66); ch. 3 .. 239(v.39); ch. 6 .. 403(v.10), 452(v.35)

experience of the divine play, ch. 6 .. 416(v.17)

experience, outer, ch. 2 .. 158(v.58); ch. 5 .. 328(intro.) 364 (v.21), 371-372(v.24), 376-377(v.27); ch. 6 .. 393(v.4)

experience, process of, ch. 3 .. 206(v.15), 219(v.26); ch. 5 .. 365(v.21)

experience, quality of, ch. 6 .. 442(v.29)

experience, sensory, ch. 2 .. 121(v.41); ch. 3 .. 237(v.37); ch. 5 .. 362(v.20); ch. 6 .. 425(v.21)

experience, trinity of, ch. 3 .. 206(v.15); ch. 6 .. 394(v.4)

experienced (object of experience), ch. 3 .. 206(v.15)

experiencer, ch. 2 .. 98(v.18); ch. 3 .. 206(v.15); ch. 5 .. 343-344(v.8,9)

external activity, ch. 6 .. 430(v.24)

extinction of ignorance, ch. 4 .. 264(v.8)

extremes (see also opposites), ch. 5 .. 327-328(intro.)

eyebrows, ch. 5 .. 376-377(v.27)

faculty of experience, ch. 6 .. 437(v.27)

failures in life, ch. 1 .. 63-64(v.39); ch. 4 .. 318(v.40)

faith, ch. 2 .. 85-86(v.7); ch. 3 .. 227(v.31); ch. 4 .. 316-319 (v.39-40); ch. 6 .. 456(v.37), 467(v.47)

faith and knowledge, relationship of, ch. 4 .. 318-319(v.40)

faith, lack of, ch. 4 .. 318-319(v.40)

faith, three fields of, ch. 4 .. 316-317(v.39)

fallen from both — human and divine, ch. 6 .. 458(v.38)

fame, ch. 2 .. 110-111(v.33-34)

fame, ill, ch. 2 .. 110-112(v.34-36)

family, ch. 1 .. 62-70(v.38-45); ch. 3 .. 192(v.8)

family *dharma,* ch. 1 .. 64-70(v.40-45); ch. 2 .. 84-85(v.7)

family disorder, ch. 1 .. 69(v.44)

family of *yogis,* ch. 6 .. 461(v.42)

family profession, ch. 1 .. 69(v.44)

family traditions, ch. 1 .. 66-69(v.42-44)

fatalism, ch. 2 .. 171(v.70)

fault-finding, ch. 3 .. 227-228(v.31-32)

fear, ch. 1 .. 50(v.28); ch. 2 .. 117-119(v.40), 154-155(v.56); ch. 4 .. 265-266(v.10), 315(v.38), 320(v.41); ch. 5 .. 377-379(v.28-29); ch. 6 .. 406(v.12), 409-410(v.14), 456(v.37)

fear, loss of, ch. 2 .. 154-155(v.56)

feeding the senses, ch. 2 .. 159-161(v.59); ch. 4 .. 294(v.26), 298(v.30); ch. 6 .. 414-415(v.16)

feeling (see also emotion), ch. 3 .. 221(v.27); ch. 4 .. 303(v.34), 315(v.38); ch. 6 .. 412(v.14), 434(v.25), 443(v.30), 448(v.32)

feeling, most refined qualities of, ch. 4 .. 315(v.38)

feeling of want (see also desire), ch. 4 .. 284(v.19)

fight (see also battle, war, warrior), ch. 2 .. 108-110(v.31-33), 113-114(v.37-38); ch. 3 .. 180(v.1)

finer levels of the senses, ch. 2 .. 160(v.59), 162(v.61), 168-169(v.68)

finest activity, ch. 3 .. 211(v.19); ch. 4 .. 313(v.38), 315(v.38); ch. 5 .. 332(v.2), 348(v.11)

finest aspect of individual life, ch. 6 .. 423(v.20)

finest aspect of subjectivity, ch. 2 .. 164(v.63)

finest intellect, ch. 2 .. 151(v.55)

fire, ch. 6 .. 384(v.1), 387(v.1)

fire of knowledge, ch. 4 .. 281-285(v.19), 308-311(v.36-37)

fire of *Yoga,* ch. 4 .. 295-296(v.27)

first manifestation of creation, ch. 3 .. 206(v.15)

five conditions for meditation, ch. 6 .. 402-405(v.10)

five elements, ch. 6 .. 424-425(v.21)

five factors for accomplishment of action, ch. 2 .. 153(v.55)

five levels of action, ch. 3 .. 212(v.19)

five organs of action, ch. 3 .. 190(v.7)

five senses of perception, ch. 3 .. 190(v.7)

fixity in *Brahman,* ch. 4 .. 290-292(v.24)

flashes, ch. 6 .. 450(v.33)

flexibility, ch. 6 .. 439(v.28)

flow of desire, ch. 1 .. 51(v.28), 56(v.32); ch. 3 .. 236(v.37), 239(v.39), 242(v.41)

flow of life, ch. 3 .. 192(v.8)

fondness, undue, ch. 2 .. 155-157(v.57)

food, ch. 3 .. 200-205(v.13-14), 221(v.27); ch. 4 .. 298-299 (v.30); ch. 6 .. 415-416(v.16)

food, earning of, ch. 3 .. 203(v.13)

food, quality of, ch. 3 .. 203(v.13)

forces, negative, ch. 1 .. 27(v.1), 38(v.15), 54(v.30); ch. 2 .. 108(v.31); ch. 4 .. 264(v.8)

forces, positive, ch. 1 .. 27(v.1), 38(v.15); ch. 2 .. 108(v.31)

forget, trying to, ch. 6 .. 405(v.10)

formation of a desire, ch. 4 .. 284(v.19)

former practice, ch. 6 .. 463(v.44)

foundation of God-consciousness, ch. 6 .. 428(v.38)

four interpretations of renunciation, ch. 5 .. 331-332(v.2)

four levels of attainment, ch. 6 .. 467(v.47)

fourfold order, ch. 4 .. 269-270(v.13); ch. 5 .. 379(v.29)

free from desires, ch. 2 .. 152(v.55); ch. 4 .. 281-284(v.19), 286-287(v.21-22); ch. 5 .. 333(v.3), 374-376(v.26), 377-378 (v.28)

free from longing, ch. 2 .. 154-155(v.56); ch. 3 .. 225(v.30)

free will (see also freedom of action), ch. 1 .. 27(v.1), 63(v.39); ch. 2 .. 104-105(v.27); ch. 4 .. 268(v.12)

freedom (see also eternal freedom, liberation), ch. 2 .. 95(v.15), 115(v.38); ch. 3 .. 180(v.1), 197-198(v.11), 202(v.13), 210 (v.19), 214(v.20), 222-223(v.28), 225(v.30), 227(v.31), 229(v.33), 231(v.34), 241(v.41), 244(v.43); ch. 4 .. 275 (v.16), 280(v.18), 288(v.22), 297(v.28); ch. 5 .. 326(intro.), 329-330(intro.-v.1), 333-334(v.3-4), 339(v.7), 347-350(v.11-13), 354-355(v.15-16); ch. 6 .. 387(v.1), 398(v.6), 420 (v.18), 427(v.23), 461(v.41)

freedom from the bondage of action, ch. 3 .. 187(v.4), 218(v.25); ch. 5 .. 349(v.12)

freedom of action (see also free will), ch. 1 .. 63(v.39); ch. 2 .. 104-105(v.27); ch. 3 .. 180(v.1), 233(v.35); ch. 4 .. 268 (v.12)

freedom, prerequisite to, ch. 3 .. 227(v.31)

friend, ch. 5 .. 388(v.29); ch. 6 .. 395-399(v.5-6)

friend, his own, ch. 6 .. 395-399(v.5-6)

front of his nose, ch. 6 .. 408(v.13)

fruit of action, ch. 2 .. 133-135(v.47), 138-145(v.49-51); ch. 3 .. 199-200(v.12), df. 199(v.12), 225(v.30); ch. 4 .. 250 (intro.), 271-272(v.14), 280-283(v.18-19), 285-286(v.20); ch. 5 .. 348-349(v.12), 351-354(v.14-15); ch. 6 .. 384-386 (v.1)

fruit of action, quality of, ch. 5 .. 351(v.14)

fruits of *yagya,* ch. 4 .. 301(v.32)

fulfilment (see also enlightenment, realization), ch. 2 .. 130-132 (v.45-46), 163(v.61), 164(v.63), 168(v.68); ch. 3 .. 185-186(v.3), 191(v.8), 201(v.13), 206-207(v.15-16), 212(v.19), 217(v.24), 225(v.30), 227(v.31), 229(v.33), 240(v.39), 244-245(v.43); ch. 4 .. 249(intro.), 251(v.1), 264(v.8), 273(v.15), 280(v.18), 287(v.22), 302(v.33), 317(v.39); ch. 5 .. 327(intro.), 336(v.5), 353(v.14), 375(v.26), 378 (v.28), 380(v.29); ch. 6 .. 383(intro.), 385(v.1), 420(v.18), 465(v.45)

fulfilment of action, ch. 2 .. 134(v.47); ch. 3 .. 245(v.43); ch. 4 .. 268(v.12), 291(v.24), 310(v.37)

fulfilment of desire, ch. 2 .. 162-163(v.61-62); ch. 3 .. 196(v.10), 241(v.40), 245(v.43); ch. 4 .. 280(v.18)

fulfilment of *dharma,* ch. 6 .. 427(v.23)

fulfilment of Union, ch. 4 .. 321(v.42)

full development of the senses, ch. 6 .. 416(v.17)

full mental potential, ch. 2 .. 133(v.46), 162(v.61); ch. 5 .. 343 (v.8,9)

full stature of Being and activity, ch. 5 .. 349(v.12)

fullnesses, two, ch. 2 .. 79(v.2); ch. 4 .. 250-251(intro.), 256 (v.2), 262(v.7), 279(v.18); ch. 6 .. 449(v.32)

functioning of the ego, ch. 3 .. 206(v.15)

fundamental *yagya,* ch. 3 .. 201(v.13)

gain, ch. 2 .. 113-114(v.37-38), 130(v.45), 155-157(v.57); ch. 3 .. 209(v.18); ch. 4 .. 287(v.22); ch. 5 .. 332(v.2); ch. 6 .. 425-427(v.22-23)

gaze, ch. 6 .. 408(v.13)

gifts of the gods, ch. 3 .. 199(v.12)

glory of action, ch. 3 .. 205(v.14), 213(v.20)

glory of knowledge, ch. 4 .. 320(v.41); ch. 5 .. 353(v.14), 355-356(v.16)

glory of renunciation, ch. 5 .. 353(v.14), 379-380(v.29)

glory of the *Bhagavad-Gita,* ch. 6 .. 441(v.28)

glory of transcendental meditation, ch. 5 .. 344(v.8,9)

glory of *Yoga,* ch. 6 .. 426(v.22)

glow on the face, ch. 2 .. 153(v.55); ch. 6 .. 410(v.14)

goal of all actions, ch. 4 .. 302(v.33)

goal of all desires, ch. 2 .. 170(v.70)

goal of all learning, ch. 4 .. 297(v.28)

goal of *yagya,* ch. 3 .. 201(v.13); ch. 4 .. 301-302(v.32-33)

goal of *Yoga,* ch. 2 .. 118(v.40), 147(v.53); ch. 6 .. 453(v.35)

God (see also Divine, Krishna, Supreme), ch. 2 .. 131(v.45), 162-163(v.61); ch. 3 .. 185(v.3), 187-188(v.4), 193(v.8), 196(v.10), 203(v.13), 207(v.16), 210-212(v.19), 215-217(v.22-24), 226-227(v.30-31); ch. 4 .. 250(intro.), 259-273(v.5-15), 276-277(v.17), 279(v.18), 288(v.22), 296(v.27), 307-308(v.35), 313(v.38), 315-317(v.38-39); ch. 5 .. 325-326(intro.), 347(v.11), 352-353(v.14), 379-380(v.29); ch. 6 .. 386-387(v.1), 391-392(v.3), 408(v.13), 411(v.14), 416(v.17), 426(v.22), 428(v.23), 443-452(v.30-34), 457(v.38), 467-468(v.47)

God, all beings seen in, ch. 4 .. 307-308(v.35)

God and Absolute, relationship of, ch. 6 .. 444(v.30)

God and man, difference between, ch. 4 .. 259(v.5)

God and man, relationship of, ch. 6 .. 443-450(v.30-32)

God and relativity, ch. 3 .. 215(v.22)

God and the devotee, difference between, ch. 6 .. 448(v.32)

God, communion with, ch. 5 .. 380(v.29); ch. 6 .. 444(v.30)

God-consciousness, ch. 3 .. 185(v.3), 187-188(v.4), 191-193(v.8), 196(v.9), 197-198(v.11), 200-202(v.12-13), 206-207(v.15-16), 209-213(v.18-20), 226-227(v.30-31), 240(v.39); ch. 4 .. 250-251(intro.), 264(v.8), 266-267(v.10-11), 271(v.14), 273(v.15), 276-277(v.17), 279-280(v.18), 283(v.19), 288(v.22), 296-297(v.27-28), 300-302(v.31-33), 305-313(v.35-38), 315-318(v.38-39), 321(v.42); ch. 5 .. 327(intro.), 332(v.2), 334(v.3), 336(v.5), 346-349(v.11-12), 353(v.14), 367(v.22), 379-380(v.29); ch. 6 .. 383(intro.), 391-394

(v.3-4), 396-397(v.5), 410-412(v.14), 414(v.15), 426(v.22), 428(v.23), 443-456(v.30-37), 458(v.38), 461(v.42), 464-467(v.45-47)

God-consciousness, action in, ch. 6 .. 447(v.31)

God-consciousness, basis of, ch. 6 .. 452(v.34)

God-consciousness: development from cosmic consciousness, ch. 4 .. 307(v.35), 313(v.38), 315(v.38)

God-consciousness, experience in, ch. 4 .. 307-308(v.35), 316 (v.38); ch. 6 .. 448(v.32)

God-consciousness, foundation of, ch. 6 .. 458(v.38)

God-consciousness, means to attain, ch. 3 .. 211(v.19)

God-consciousness, physiology of gaining, ch. 4 .. 315(v.38)

God, enlightened man distinguished from, ch. 3 .. 215-216(v.22)

God: idea as a high ideal beyond reach, ch. 3 .. 216(v.22)

God, Incarnation of, ch. 4 .. 259-265(v.5-9)

God, knowledge of, ch. 4 .. 316(v.38); ch. 5 .. 379(v.29)

God, Life of, ch. 4 .. 308(v.35)

God, love of (see also devotion), ch. 4 .. 307(v.35)

God, man's link with, ch. 3 .. 196(v.10)

God on the level of the senses, ch. 4 .. 264(v.8); ch. 6 .. 444 (v.30), 468(v.47)

God, personal, ch. 6 .. 444-450(v.30-32)

God, play with, ch. 6 .. 449(v.32)

God, realization of (see also God-consciousness), ch. 3 .. 196 (v.10), 210(v.19); ch. 4 .. 272(v.14); ch. 5 .. 380(v.29); ch. 6 .. 444(v.30), 452(v.34)

God, seekers of, ch. 4 .. 272-273(v.15)

God, Self seen in, ch. 4 .. 307(v.35)

God, sin against, ch. 3 .. 207(v.16); ch. 6 .. 449-450(v.32)

God, surrender of action to, ch. 3 .. 226(v.30); ch. 5 .. 352-353 (v.14); ch. 6 .. 411(v.14)

God, thinking of, ch. 3 .. 185(v.3); ch. 5 .. 345(v.10); ch. 6 .. 444-445(v.30-31)

God, Union with, ch. 3 .. 187(v.4); ch. 4 .. 266(v.10), 273(v.15); ch. 5 .. 379-380(v.29); ch. 6 .. 447-450(v.32)

God, will of, ch. 6 .. 411(v.14)

Godhead, level of the, ch. 5 .. 380(v.29)

Godhead, silence of, ch. 6 .. 392(v.3)

gods, ch. 3 .. 194-195(v.9), 197-200(v.11-12), 206(v.15); ch. 4 .. 268(v.12), 292-293(v.25)

God's action, ch. 3 .. 188(v.4)

gods, blessings of the, ch. 3 .. 194-195(v.9), 197(v.11), 199(v.12); ch. 4 .. 268(v.12), 293(v.25)

God's consciousness, ch. 4 .. 268(v.11)

gods, gifts of, ch. 3 .. 199(v.12)

gods, offering to the, ch. 3 .. 198-199(v.11-12); ch. 4 .. 268(v.12), 292-293(v.25)

gods, pleasing the, ch. 3 .. 194(v.9), 198-199(v.11-12)

good action (see also right action), ch. 2 .. 111(v.34); ch. 5 .. 374(v.25)

good and evil (see also right and wrong), ch. 1 .. 35-36 (v.13), 41-42(v.19-20), 44(v.23), 50(v.28); ch. 2 .. 127(v.45), 141-143(v.50); ch. 3 .. 219(v.26), 224(v.29)

good, highest, ch. 3 .. 197-198(v.11); ch. 4 .. 278(v.17)

good, supreme, ch. 5 .. 331-332(v.2)

Govinda (master of the senses), ch. 1 .. 57(v.32); ch. 2 .. 88(v.9)

grace, ch. 2 .. 164-165(v.64-65); ch. 5 .. 350(v.13)

gradualness of development, ch. 6 .. 432-433(v.25)

great man (see also integrated man, realized man), ch. 1 .. 56-57 (v.32-33), 65(v.40); ch. 3 .. 214-215(v.21)

greatest danger to life, ch. 3 .. 233(v.35)

greatest impurity in life, ch. 4 .. 312(v.38)

greatest joy of relativity, ch. 2 .. 169(v.68)

greatest longevity, ch. 4 .. 253(v.1)

grief, ch. 1 .. 49(v.28); ch. 2 .. 87(v.8), 90-91(v.11)

grieve, ch. 2 .. 90(v.11), 102-105(v.25-27), 107(v.30); ch. 5 .. 361-363(v.20)

gross, ch. 2 .. 129(v.45), 160(v.59), 168-169(v.67-68); ch. 3 .. 194-195(v.9), 203(v.13), 205(v.14), 207(v.16), 213(v.20), 219(v.26); ch. 4 .. 266(v.10), 315(v.38); ch. 5 .. 339(v.7); ch. 6 .. 390(v.3), 405-406(v.10-11), 410(v.14), 415(v.16)

gross and subtle, ch. 2 .. 129(v.45), 160(v.59), 168-169(v.68); ch. 3 .. 195(v.9), 197(v.11), 200(v.12), 207(v.16), 213 (v.20), 219(v.26); ch. 4 .. 279(v.18); ch. 5 .. 332(v.2), 339(v.7), 360(v.19); ch. 6 .. 390(v.3), 394(v.4), 403(v.10), 421(v.19), 433(v.25)

gross aspect of *yagya,* ch. 3 .. 195(v.9), 205(v.14)

Gudakesha (Lord of Sleep), ch. 1 .. 45(v.24)

gunas, ch. 2 .. 126-132(v.45-46), df. 128-129(v.45), 160(v.59); ch. 3 .. 179(v.1), 188(v.5), 206(v.15), 219-226(v.26-30), 228(v.32), 233-240(v.35-39); ch. 4 .. 251(v.1), 262(v.7),

269-270(v.13), 274(v.16), 279(v.18), 287(v.21-22), 291 (v.24), 296(v.27), 306-307(v.35), 311-312(v.38); ch. 5 .. 330(v.1), 342(v.8,9), 352(v.14), 354(v.14), 357(v.17), 374 (v.25); ch. 6 .. 424(v.21)

gunas, basis of the, ch. 3 .. 234(v.35); ch. 4 .. 270(v.13)

gunas, dharma of the, ch. 3 .. 233-234(v.35)

gunas, knowledge of the, ch. 3 .. 222(v.28)

Gyana Kanda (pertaining to knowledge), ch. 2 .. 123(v.42); ch. 3 .. 195(v.9)

GyanaYoga (the path of Union through knowledge), ch. 2 .. 131 (v.45); ch. 3 .. 183-186(v.3), 244(v.43)

gyani (one who is successful on the path of knowledge), ch. 2 .. 86(v.7), 131(v.45)

habit, ch. 2 .. 174(v.72)

happier life, ch. 6 .. 460-461(v.41)

happiness (see also enjoyment, pleasure), ch. 1 .. 61-62(v.36-37); ch. 2 .. 118-119(v.40), 121(v.41), 157(v.57), 161-162(v.60-61), 165-169(v.66-68), 170(v.70); ch. 3 .. 196(v.10), 199 (v.12), 207(v.16), 229(v.33), 239(v.39); ch. 4 .. 267(v.11), 315(v.38), 318-319(v.40); ch. 5 .. 333(v.3), 336(v.5), 343 (v.8,9), 350(v.13), 364-368(v.21-23), 370-372(v.23-24), 380(v.29); ch. 6 .. 403-405(v.10), 409(v.14), 415(v.17), 419(v.18), 424(v.20), 427(v.23), 431-432(v.24-25), 436 (v.26), 455(v.36)

happiness, degree of, ch. 2 .. 119(v.40); ch. 5 .. 367(v.22); ch. 6 .. 461(v.41)

happiness, eternal, ch. 5 .. 364-368(v.21-22); ch. 6 .. 441(v.28)

happiness, expansion of, ch. 1 .. 62(v.37); ch. 3 .. 236(v.37); ch. 5 .. 352(v.14), 380(v.29); ch. 6 .. 415(v.16)

happiness, experience of, ch. 2 .. 121(v.41), 166(v.66); ch. 3 .. 239(v.39); ch. 6 .. 403(v.10), 452(v.35)

happiness, search for, ch. 2 .. 118-119(v.40), 121(v.41), 133 (v.46), 166(v.66); ch. 3 .. 239(v.39); ch. 4 .. 267(v.11); ch. 5 .. 333(v.3), 371(v.24)

happiness, supreme, ch. 3 .. 229(v.33); ch. 5 .. 380(v.29); ch. 6 .. 428(v.33), 436-438(v.26-27)

harmony, ch. 3 .. 179(v.1), 191(v.8), 195-198(v.9-11), 202(v.13), 214(v.20), 244(v.43); ch. 4 .. 276(v.17), 317(v.39); ch. 5 .. 329(intro.), 340(v.7), 372(v.24), 375(v.26); ch. 6 .. 391(v.3), 416-417(v.17), 440(v.28), 446(v.31), 461(v.41)

harmony with the laws of nature, ch. 2 .. 133(v.46); ch. 3 .. 205 (v.14); ch. 5 .. 333(v.3), 345(v.10)

Hatha Yoga, ch. 6 . . 390(v.3)

heart, ch.1 . . 49-54(v.28-30), 58(v.34), 60-61(v.36), 71(v.47);
    ch. 2 . . 76-77(v.1), 81(v.3), 127(v.45), 146(v.52), 150
    (v.55), 155-157(v.56-57), 162(v.61), 165(v.65); ch. 3 . .
    180(v.1), 214(v.20), 240(v.39); ch. 4 . . 264(v.8), 286(v.21),
    303(v.34), 307(v.35), 317-318(v.39), 321-322(v.42); ch. 6
    . . 400(v.8), 426(v.22), 447(v.32)

heart and mind, ch. 1 . . 49-55(v.28-31), 57-58(v.33), 60-61(v.36),
    71(v.47); ch. 2 . . 76-77(v.1), 127(v.45), 150(v.55), 165
    (v.65); ch. 3 . . 240(v.39); ch. 4 . . 286(v.21), 303(v.34),
    306(v.35), 317-318(v.39), 322(v.42); ch. 6 . . 400(v.8),
    444(v.30)

heart and mind, communication between, ch. 1 . . 51(v.28)

heart and mind, coordination of, ch.1 . . 49-54(v.28-30)

heart, purity of, ch. 1 . . 55(v.31)

heart, sorrow in, ch. 2 . . 155(v.56)

heaven, ch. 2 . . 109(v.32); ch. 3 . . 198(v.11); ch. 5 . . 380(v.29)

height of realization, ch. 6 . . 449(v.32)

higher powers, contacting, ch. 3 . . 195(v.9); ch. 4 . . 268(v.12)

higher powers of nature, ch. 3 . . 194-195(v.9), 198-201(v.11-13),
    205(v.14)

highest capacity of the senses, ch. 5 . . 343(v.8,9)

highest civilization, ch. 4 . . 254(v.1)

highest good, ch. 3 . . 197-198(v.11); ch. 4 . . 278(v.17)

highest level of consciousness, ch. 6 . . 460(v.41)

highest state of evolution, ch. 3 . . 196(v.10); ch. 6 . . 467-468
    (v.47)

highest type of activity, ch. 3 . . 211(v.19)

highest *yogi,* ch. 6 . . 447-450(v.32)

Hindu aims of life, ch. 6 . . 427-428(v.23)

history, ch. 4 . . 252-255(v.1-2); ch. 6 . . 444(v.30), 468(v.47)

history, Indian conception of, ch. 4 . . 252-255(v.1)

history of the *Bhagavad-Gita,* ch. 4 . . 252-258(v.1-3)

holy tradition, ch. 4 . . 257-258(v.2-3)

homage, ch. 4 . . 303-305(v.34)

horizontal plane, ch. 2 . . 134(v.47)

householder, ch. 2 . . 149(v.54), 152-153(v.55), 157(v.57); ch. 3 . .
    183-186(v.3), 244-245(v.43); ch. 4 . . 249(intro.); ch. 5 . .
    329(intro.), 235(v.5), 348(v.11); ch. 6 . . 384-388(intro.-
    v.2)

Hrishikesha (Lord of the senses; one with long hair), ch. 1 . . 37 (v.15)

human and divine, ch. 5 . . 362(v.20)

human and divine, fallen from both, ch. 6 . . 458(v.38)

humility, ch. 5 . . 358-359(v.18)

hypocrisy, ch. 2 . . 94(v.15), 134(v.47), 139(v.49); ch. 3 . . 189 (v.6); ch. 6 . . 386(v.1)

"I", ch. 2 . . 171-172(v.71); ch. 3 . . 220-221(v.27), 225(v.30); ch. 5 . . 352(v.14), 355(v.16); ch. 6 . . 422(v.19)

idea of restraint, ch. 3 . . 231(v.34)

identified with desires, ch. 2 . . 151(v.55)

identify, ch. 2 . . 159(v.58); ch. 4 . . 321(v.41); ch. 5 . . 370(v.23)

idleness, ch. 3 . . 187(v.4)

ignorance (see also bondage), ch. 2 . . 78(v.2), 81(v.3), 95(v.15), 119(v.40), 169-170(v.69); ch. 3 . . 202(v.13), 218-221(v.26-27), 224(v.29), 244(v.43); ch. 4 . . 250(intro.), 266(v.10), 274(v.16), 287(v.21), 309(v.36), 312(v.38), 318-319(v.40), 321-322(v.42); ch. 5 . . 334(v.4), 352-355(v.14-16), 359-360 (v.18), 367(v.22); ch. 6 . . 428(v.23), 458(v.38), 460(v.41)

ignorance, action in, ch. 3 . . 217-218(v.25)

ignorance, desire in, ch. 3 . . 237(v.37)

ignorance, destruction of, ch. 5 . . 355(v.16)

ignorance, extinction of, ch. 4 . . 264(v.8)

ignorant, teaching the, ch. 3 . . 218-220(v.26), 224(v.29)

ill fame, ch. 2 . . 110-112(v.34-36)

illusion, ch. 2 . . 81(v.3)

imagination, ch. 3 . . 199(v.12); ch. 6 . . 446(v.31)

immortality (see also eternal life, imperishable), ch. 2 . . 91-92 (v.12), 94-95(v.15), 101(v.23)

impartial discrimination (see also discrimination), ch. 3 . . 185(v.3)

impartial divine nature, ch. 2 . . 84(v.7)

imperishable (see also eternal life, immorality), ch. 2 . . 92(v.12), 115(v.38), 128(v.45); ch. 3 . . 179-180(v.1), 205-207(v.15); ch. 4 . . 251(v.1), 255(v.2), 261(v.6); ch. 5 . . 334(v.4); ch. 6 . . 440(v.28)

impersonal, ch. 6 . . 446-447(v.31-32)

importance of action, ch. 4 . . 301(v.32)

impractical, ch. 6 . . 453(v.35)

impression, ch. 2 . . 117(v.39), 142-143(v.50), 156(v.57), 158 (v.58); ch. 3 . . 190(v.7), 218(v.25); ch. 4 . . 284-287(v.19-

21), 311(v.37); ch. 5 .. 341(v.7), 343(v.8,9), 362(v.20), 365(v.21); ch. 6 .. 422(v.19)

impressions, storehouse of, ch. 4 .. 281-287(v.19-21), 311(v.37); ch. 6 .. 422(v.19)

impulse of a thought, ch. 4 .. 284(v.19)

impurity, ch. 1 .. 66(v.41); ch. 3 .. 227(v.31); ch. 4 .. 312(v.38)

impurity, greatest, ch. 4 .. 312(v.38)

inability to fulfill one's desires, ch. 2 .. 163(v.62)

inaction, ch. 2 .. 133-135(v.47); ch. 3 .. 191-193(v.8); ch. 4 .. 274-283(v.16-19); ch. 5 .. 329-331(v.1)

inactivity of deep sleep, ch. 3 .. 187(v.4)

Incarnation of God, ch. 4 .. 259-265(v.5-9)

incarnation of man, ch. 4 .. 259(v.5)

Incarnation of the Absolute, ch. 4 .. 261(v.6)

incentive of desire, ch. 4 .. 284-285(v.19); ch. 6 .. 388-389(v.2), 393-394(v.4)

incentive to action, ch. 6 .. 429-430(v.24)

inception of the thinking process, ch. 2 .. 140(v.49)

increasing charm (see also natural tendency of the mind), ch. 2 .. 119(v.40), 121(v.41), 166(v.66), 169(v.68); ch. 4 .. 317 (v.39); ch. 5 .. 332(v.2); ch. 6 .. 403-404(v.10), 409-411 (v.14), 413(v.15), 436(v.26)

independent of possessions, ch. 2 .. 126-132(v.45); ch. 4 .. 286-287(v.21)

indestructible, ch. 2 .. 96-97(v.17), 99(v.21), 101(v.23)

India, ch. 2 .. 171(v.70); ch. 4 .. 252(v.1), 257(v.2)

Indian conception of history and time, ch. 4 .. 252-255(v.1)

indifference, ch. 2 .. 134(v.47), 139(v.49), 146(v.52); ch. 4 .. 256(v.2); ch. 5 .. 340(v.7); ch. 6 .. 411(v.14)

individual *dharma,* ch. 1 .. 70(v.45)

individual ego, ch. 2 .. 172(v.71); ch. 3 .. 206(v.15), 221(v.27); ch. 5 .. 343(v.8,9)

individual existence, regaining of, ch. 6 .. 464(v.45)

individual life (see also individuality), ch. 1 .. 63(v.39); ch. 2 .. 98(v.18), 143(v.51), 173(v.72); ch. 3 .. 187(v.4), 197 (v.11), 204(v.14), 234(v.35); ch. 4 .. 250(intro.), 279 (v.18), 296(v.27); ch. 5 .. 325(intro.), 346-347(v.11), 353 (v.14), 357(v.17); ch. 6 .. 387(v.1), 392(v.3), 396(v.5), 416(v.17), 430(v.24), 464(v.45)

individual life, finest aspect of, ch. 6 .. 423(v.20)

individual mind, ch. 6 .. 437(v.27)

individual, prosperity of the, ch. 3 .. 196(v.10), 199-200(v.12)

individual responsibility, ch. 6 .. 395-397(v.5)

individuality (see also individual life), ch. 2 .. 96-98(v.17-18), 142(v.50), 171-173(v.71-72); ch. 3 .. 201-202(v.13), 209 (v.18); ch. 4 .. 292(v.24), 303(v.34), 313(v.38), 318(v.39); ch. 5 .. 339-340(v.7), 350(v.13), 374(v.25); ch. 6 .. 410 (v.14), 419(v.18), 421-422(v.19-20), 433(v.25), 437(v.27), 448(v.32)

individuality, limitations of, ch. 3 .. 234(v.35); ch. 5 .. 350(v.13)

inertia, ch. 3 .. 207(v.15)

infinite joy, ch. 6 .. 424-425(v.21), 439-441(v.28)

influence in the atmosphere, ch. 4 .. 276(v.17)

influence, life-damaging (see also negative influence), ch. 4 .. 277(v.17)

influence, life-supporting (see also positive influence), ch. 3 .. 198 (v.11), 200-202(v.12-13), 204(v.14), 214(v.20); ch. 4 .. 276(v.17), 289(v.23), 309(v.36); ch. 5 .. 345(v.10); ch. 6 .. 439(v.28)

influence, negative (see also life-damaging influence), ch. 1 .. 60 (v.36); ch. 2 .. 143(v.50); ch. 3 .. 227(v.31)

influence of action, ch. 2 .. 100(v.21), 137(v.48), 142-143(v.50); ch. 3 .. 197-198(v.11); ch. 4 .. 274(v.16); ch. 5 .. 350 (v.13), 354(v.15)

influence of action, mechanics of, ch. 3 .. 197-198(v.11)

influence of desire, ch. 3 .. 239(v.39)

influence of past actions (see also action-reaction, *karma*), ch. 4 .. 259(v.5), 311(v.37)

influence of the senses, ch. 6 .. 421(v.19), 451(v.34)

influence, positive (see also life-supporting influence), ch. 2 .. 143(v.50)

influence, social, ch. 2 .. 110-11(v.33-34)

influence, waves of, ch. 4 .. 276(v.17)

infusion of Being, ch. 2 .. 144(v.51), 173(v.72); ch. 3 .. 211 (v.19), 214(v.20); ch. 4 .. 283(v.19), 291(v.24), 312-313 (v.38), 317(v.39); ch. 5 .. 340-341(v.7), 344(v.10), 350 (v.13), 363(v.20), 369-370(v.23); ch. 6 .. 386(v.1), 391 (v.3), 400(v.8), 405(v.10), 412(v.14), 436(v.26), 442(v.29), 453(v.35), 462(v.43), 467(v.47)

inner aspect of life, ch. 2 .. 92(v.12), 95(v.15)

inner awareness, ch. 3 .. 187(v.4)

inner creative silence, ch. 2 .. 136(v.48)

inner state, ch. 2 .. 153(v.55)

innocence in transcendental meditation, ch. 6 .. 411(v.14), 432-433(v.25)

inquiry, ch. 4 .. 303-305(v.34)

insatiable desire, ch. 3 .. 238-240(v.39)

instrument of the Divine, ch. 4 .. 287(v.22); ch. 5 .. 346(v.11)

integrated life, philosophy of, ch. 5 .. 328(intro.)

integrated man (see also *jivan-mukti,* realized man), ch. 2 .. 86 (v.7), 135(v.48), 164(v.64); ch. 3 .. 211(v.19), 213(v.20); ch. 4 .. 252(v.1)

integration, ch. 3 .. 186(v.3), 192(v.8), 209(v.18), 213(v.20), 245(v.43); ch. 4 .. 255(v.2); ch. 5 .. 338-339(v.7), 372 (v.24); ch. 6 .. 386(v.1)

integration of functions of the nervous system, ch. 4 .. 315(v.38)

intellect, ch. 2 .. 107(v.29), 116-117(v.39), 138-159(v.49-58), 161-170(v.61-69); ch. 3 .. 186(v.3), 204(v.14), 219(v.26), 223(v.28), 226(v.30), 240-244(v.39-43); ch. 4 .. 249(intro.), 304(v.34), 320(v.41); ch. 5 .. 326(intro.), 339(v.7), 345-348(v.10-11), 356-357(v.17), 372(v.24), 377(v.28); ch. 6 .. 401(v.9), 423-425(v.20-21), 432-434(v.25), 462(v.43), 468 (v.47)

intellect, absolute state of, ch. 2 .. 140(v.49)

intellect, balanced, ch. 2 .. 138-141(v.49)

intellect, beyond the, ch. 3 .. 243-245(v.42-43); ch. 6 .. 425(v.21)

intellect, destruction of, ch. 2 .. 163-164(v.63)

intellect, established (see also balanced intellect, steady intellect), ch. 2 .. 155-162(v.55-61), 165-167(v.66), 168-171(v.68-70); ch. 3 .. 180(v.1), 206(v.15), 209(v.18); ch. 5 .. 361 (v.19)

intellect, finest, ch. 2 .. 151(v.55)

intellect, principle of, ch. 6 .. 424(v.21)

intellect, resolute (see also established intellect), ch. 2 .. 121-122 (v.41), 124-126(v.44-45), 147(v.53), 168(v.68); ch. 3 .. 179(v.1); ch. 6 .. 399(v.7), 423(v.20)

intellect, steady (see also balanced intellect), ch. 2 .. 148-161 (v.54-59); ch. 5 .. 361-363(v.20); ch. 6 .. 422-424(v.19-20)

intellect, undeveloped, ch. 5 .. 335(v.5)

intellect, uninvolved, ch. 2 .. 138(v.49)

intellect, wavering, ch. 2 .. 151(v.55)

intellectual alertness, ch. 4 .. 304(v.34)

intellectual analysis during transcendental meditation, ch. 6 .. 433(v.25)

intellectual clarity, ch. 1 .. 64(v.39)

intellectual conception of Reality, ch. 2 .. 100(v.21), 103(v.25),
    106-107(v.29); ch. 5 .. 363(v.20); ch. 6 .. 400(v.8)

intellectual understanding (see also knowledge, understanding),
    ch. 2 .. 100(v.21), 103(v.25), 106-107(v.29), 116-117(v.39),
    152(v.55); ch. 3 .. 177(intro.), 180(v.1), 185(v.3), 219
    (v.26), 222-224(v.28-29), 227(v.31), 239(v.39); ch. 4 ..
    274(v.16), 320(v.41); ch. 5 .. 363(v.20)

intelligence, ch. 3 .. 196(v.10), 206(v.15); ch. 4 .. 270(v.13), 300
    (v.31); ch. 5 .. 354(v.15), 367(v.22)

intelligence, cosmic, ch. 2 .. 118(v.40), 137(v.48), 142(v.50);
    ch. 4 .. 268(v.11), 304(v.34); ch. 5 .. 346-347(v.11), 365
    (v.21); ch. 6 .. 393(v.3), 397-398(v.6), 416(v.17)

intelligence, creative, ch. 1 .. 66(v.41)

intensity of thought, ch. 6 .. 432(v.25)

interest, ch. 6 .. 446(v.31)

intermixture of castes, ch. 1 .. 66(v.41), 68(v.43)

internal activity, ch. 6 .. 430(v.24)

intimacy with the Creator, ch. 3 .. 225-226(v.30)

inward activity, ch. 3 .. 213(v.20); ch. 4 .. 292(v.24)

inward stroke of meditation, ch. 3 .. 193(v.8), 214(v.20), 225
    (v.30); ch. 4 .. 313(v.38); ch. 5 .. 340(v.7), 344(v.10);
    ch. 6 .. 409-411(v.14), 430-431(v.24), 434-436(v.25-26),
    438(v.27)

irresolute mind, ch. 2 .. 121-125(v.41-44)

jiva (dweller in the body), ch. 2 .. 98(v.18), 100(v.22)

jivan-mukti (man of cosmic consciousness), ch. 2 .. 132(v.46),
    145(v.51); ch. 3 .. 223(v.28), 321(v.42); ch. 5 .. 376(v.26);
    ch. 6 .. 402(v.10)

joy, infinite, ch. 6 .. 424-425(v.21), 439-441(v.28)

joys of the senses, ch. 5 .. 365-368(v.21-22)

junction-point of relativity and the Absolute, ch. 6 .. 437-438(v.27)

Kali-Yuga, ch. 4 .. 254(v.1)

Kalpa (one day of *Brahma*), ch. 4 .. 253-255(v.1)

kama (desire), ch. 6 .. 427(v.23)

karma (action), ch. 1 .. 44(v.23); ch. 2 .. 138-145(v.49-51); ch.
    3 .. 177(intro.), 179(v.1), 203(v.13), 205(v.15), 223(v.28),
    244(v.43)

karma, binding influence of (see also binding influence of action),
    ch. 3 .. 203(v.13)

Karma Kanda (Vedic exposition of *karma*), ch. 1 .. 67(v.42); ch. 2 .. 122-125(v.42-44); ch. 3 .. 195(v.9)

Karma-Sanyasa Yoga (the Yoga of action and renunciation of action), ch. 5 .. 380(v.29)

Karma Yoga (the Yoga of action), ch. 2 .. 131(v.45), 144(v.51), 149-150(v.54); ch. 3 .. 177-178(intro.), 183-186(v.3), 190 (v.7), 210(v.19), 213(v.20), 223(v.28), 243-245(v.43); ch. 4 .. 251(v.1), 290(v.1), 290(v.23), 319-322(v.41-42); ch. 5 .. 325-328(intro.), 332-333(v.2), 335(v.4); ch. 6 .. 385-388(v.1-2), 401(v.9), 420(v.18)

Karma Yoga and *Sanyasa,* prerequisite of, ch. 6 .. 387(v.1)

Karma Yoga, purpose of, ch. 5 .. 332(v.2)

Karma Yoga, superiority of, ch. 5 .. 332-333(v.2)

karma yogi, ch. 2 .. 131(v.45); ch. 3 .. 190(v.7); ch. 6 .. 385 (v.1), 387(v.1)

Keshava (one with long hair), ch. 2 .. 148-149(v.54)

killing, ch. 1 .. 55(v.31), 60-62(v.36-37); ch. 2 .. 114(v.38)

knower of *Brahman,* ch. 5 .. 361-363(v.20)

knowingness, ch. 4 .. 312(v.38)

knowledge (see also intellectual understanding), ch. 1 .. 66(v.41); ch. 2 .. 78(v.2), 85(v.7), 95(v.15), 115(v.38), 125(v.44), 128(v.45), 131(v.45), 147-148(v.53); ch. 3 .. 178-181(v.1), 183(v.3), 195(v.9), 205(v.15), 221-223(v.28), 225-226 (v.30), 228-230(v.32-33), 239(v.39), 241-242(v.41), 244 (v.43); ch. 4 .. 249-250(intro.), 252(v.1), 266(v.10), 271-275(v.14-16), 277-279(v.17-18), 281(v.19), 297(v.28), 300-312(v.32-38), 315-316(v.38-39), 318-322(v.39-42); ch. 5 .. 326-327(intro.), 342(v.8,9), 353-357(v.14-17), 368-369 (v.23), 372(v.24), 374-375(v.25-26), 379(v.29); ch. 6 .. 385(v.1), 390(v.3), 400-401(v.8), 456(v.37), 459(v.39)

knowledge, absolute state of, ch. 4 .. 312(v.38)

knowledge, all, ch. 3 .. 228(v.32)

knowledge and *dharma,* relationship between, ch. 3 .. 181(v.1)

knowledge and experience (see also experience, direct experience, intellectual understanding), ch. 2 .. 106(v.29), 116-117 (v.39), 146-148(v.52-53), 152(v.55); ch. 3 .. 177-178(intro.), 219(v.26), 222-223(v.28); ch. 4 .. 249-250(intro.), 271-272(v.14), 300-303(v.32-33), 320(v.41), 322(v.42); ch. 5 .. 326(intro.), 334(v.4), 342(v.8,9), 363(v.20); ch. 6 .. 385 (v.1), 400(v.8), 427(v.23)

knowledge and faith, relationship of, ch. 4 .. 318-319(v.40)

knowledge and realization, destroyer of, ch. 3 .. 241-242(v.41)

knowledge, benefits of, ch. 4 .. 277(v.17)

knowledge, fire of, ch. 4 .. 281-285(v.19), 308-311(v.36-37)

knowledge, glory of, ch. 4 .. 320(v.41); ch. 5 .. 353(v.14), 355-356(v.16)

knowledge, lack of (see also ignorance), ch. 4 .. 318-319(v.40); ch. 5 .. 356(v.16); ch. 6 .. 444(v.30), 457(v.38), 464(v.45)

knowledge, man of, ch. 6 .. 465-466(v.46)

knowledge of action, ch. 4 .. 274-281(v.16-18), 308(v.36); ch. 5 .. 352(v.14)

knowledge of God, ch. 4 .. 316(v.38); ch. 5 .. 379(v.29)

knowledge of renunciation (see also renunciation), ch. 5 .. 325-326(intro.), 353(v.14)

knowledge of the Divine, ch. 4 .. 308(v.36); ch. 5 .. 354(v.15)

knowledge of three *gunas*, ch. 3 .. 222(v.28)

knowledge of *yagya*, ch. 4 .. 301(v.32)

knowledge, prerequisite to, ch. 4 .. 316(v.39)

knowledge, supreme, ch. 4 .. 255(v.1), 315-316(v.38); ch. 5 .. 354(v.15)

knowledge, sword of, ch. 4 .. 321-322(v.42)

knowledge, theoretical, ch. 4 .. 300-301(v.32); ch. 6 .. 466(v.46)

knowledge, *yagya of,* ch. 4 .. 301-303(v.33)

knowledge, Yoga of, ch. 3 .. 183-186(v.3)

Krishna, ch. 1 .. 37-39(v.14-15); ch. 2 .. 89(v.10), 161-163(v.61), 166(v.66); ch. 3 .. 215-217(v.22-24), 225-228(v.30-32); ch.4 .. 258-272(v.4-14); ch. 5 .. 328(intro.), 379-380(v.29); ch. 6 .. 409-414(v.14-15), 443-449(v.30-32), 467-468(v.47)

Krishna, action of, ch. 3 .. 215-217(v.22-24); ch. 4 .. 264-265 (v.9)

Krishna, authority of, ch. 4 .. 260(v.5)

Krishna, birth of, ch. 4 .. 258-265(v.4-9)

Krishna, nature of, ch. 4 .. 260-261(v.6), 272-273(v.14-15)

Krishna, Royal Yoga of, ch. 6 .. 383(intro.)

Krishna, twofold purpose of, ch. 4 .. 263-264(v.8)

Krishna's power of creation, ch. 4 .. 260-261(v.6)

kshatriya (warrior), ch. 2 .. 108-109(v.31-32); ch. 3 .. 181(v.1), 192(v.8); ch. 4 .. 252(v.1)

Kutastha (the Immovable, the Rocklike), ch. 2 .. 151(v.55)

lack of Being, ch. 6 .. 450-451(v.33-34)

lack of experience, ch. 6 .. 464(v.45)

lack of faith, ch. 4 . . 318-319(v.40)

lack of knowledge (see also ignorance), ch. 4 . . 318-319(v.40); ch. 5 . . 356(v.16); ch. 6 . . 444(v.30), 457(v.38), 464(v.45)

lack of practice, ch. 6 . . 465(v.45)

law and order, ch. 3 . . 241(v.41); ch. 4 . . 252(v.1), 261-262 (v.6-7)

law, cosmic, ch. 1 . . 63-64(v.39); ch. 2 . . 133(v.46); ch. 5 . . 333(v.3)

laws of evolution, ch. 1 . . 68(v.43); ch. 4 . . 273(v.15)

laws of nature (see also cosmic law), ch. 1 . . 63(v.39); ch. 2 . . 123(v.42), 133(v.46); ch. 3 . . 191-192(v.8), 195(v.9), 197-198(v.11), 205(v.14), 242(v.41); ch. 4 . . 276-277(v.17), 284(v.19), 308(v.36); ch. 5 . . 375(v.26); ch. 6 . . 392(v.3), 416-417(v.17), 427(v.23), 430-431(v.24), 438-439(v.27-28)

laws of nature, harmony with, ch. 2 . . 133(v.46); ch. 3 . . 205 (v.14); ch. 5 . . 333(v.3), 345(v.10)

learning (see also master-pupil relationship, teaching), ch. 2 . . 120(v.11)

learning, goal of all, ch. 4 . . 297(v.28)

least purity, ch. 6 . . 461(v.41)

legal, ch. 3 . . 203(v.13)

length of life, ch. 6 . . 460-461(v.41)

level of consciousness (see also level of evolution), ch. 2 . . 107 (v.29), 155(v.56), 167(v.66); ch. 3 . . 186(v.3), 232(v.35); ch. 4 . . 276(v.17), 282-284(v.19), 288(v.22), 291(v.24), 299(v.31), 302(v.33), 314(v.38), 316(v.39); ch. 5 . . 367 (v.22), 380(v.29); ch. 6 . . 383(intro.), 396-397(v.5), 421 (v.19), 442-446(v.29-31), 449(v.32), 457-458(v.38), 460 (v.41)

level of consciousness, highest, ch. 6 . . 460(v.41)

level of evolution (see also level of consciousness), ch. 3 . . 195 (v.9), 232-234(v.35); ch. 4 . . 276(v.17); ch. 5 . . 352(v.14); ch. 6 . . 396(v.5), 410(v.14), 448(v.32)

level of the Godhead, ch. 5 . . 380(v.29)

levels of activity, ch. 4 . . 315(v.38)

liberation (see also eternal freedom, freedom), ch. 2 . . 115(v.38), 143-145(v.51), 174(v.72); ch. 3 . . 210(v.19), 213(v.20), 218(v.25), 222-223(v.28), 227(v.31); ch. 4 . . 249(intro.), 272-273(v.14-15), 274-275(v.16), 279(v.18), 287-289(v.22-23), 291(v.24), 305(v.34); ch. 5 . . 327-328(intro.), 334-336(v.4-5), 338-341(v.7), 356(v.17), 372(v.24), 377-378 (v.28); ch. 6 . . 385(v.1), 412-414(v.15), 428(v.23), 439 (v.28), 458(v.38), 460-461(v.41), 465(v.45)

liberation, mechanics of, ch. 4 .. 285-287(v.20-21)

liberation, perfect, ch. 6 .. 448(v.32)

liberation, seekers of, ch. 4 .. 272-273(v.15)

liberation, supreme, ch. 6 .. 412-414(v.15)

life, ch. 3 .. 178-180(v.1); ch. 5 .. 357(v.17)

life, balance in, ch. 6 .. 400(v.8)

life, beginning of (see also source of creation), ch. 3 .. 207(v.16)

life, complete success in, ch. 3 .. 197(v.11)

life, cosmic, ch. 1 .. 63(v.39); ch. 2 .. 98(v.18), 143(v.51); ch. 3 ..
        187(v.4), 197(v.11), 202-203(v.13), 234(v.35); ch. 4 ..
        250(intro.), 276(v.17), 279(v.18), 296(v.27), 315(v.38);
        ch. 5 .. 325(intro.), 346(v.11), 353(v.14); ch. 6 .. 392(v.3)

life-damaging influence (see also negative influence), ch. 4 ..
        277(v.17)

life, essential feature of, ch. 5 .. 369(v.23)

life, eternal (see also immortality), ch. 2 .. 92(v.12-13), 94-95
        (v.15), 99(v.20), 144-145(v.51), 163(v.61); ch. 3 .. 195
        (v.9), 200(v.12), 205(v.15), 226(v.30); ch. 4 .. 253(v.1),
        265(v.9); ch. 6 .. 392-393(v.3), 425(v.21), 445(v.30), 449
        (v.32), 460(v.41)

life, flow of, ch. 3 .. 192(v.8)

life, greatest danger to, ch. 3 .. 233(v.35)

life, happier, ch. 6 .. 460-461(v.41)

life, Hindu aims of, ch. 6 .. 427-428(v.23)

life, individual (see also individuality), ch. 1 .. 63(v.39); ch. 2 ..
        98(v.18), 143(v.51), 173(v.72); ch. 3 .. 187(v.4), 197(v.11),
        204(v.14), 234(v.35); ch. 4 .. 250(intro.), 279(v.18), 296
        (v.27); ch. 5 .. 325(intro.), 346-347(v.11), 353(v.14), 357
        (v.17); ch. 6 .. 387(v.1), 392(v.3), 396(v.5), 416(v.17),
        430(v.24), 464(v.45)

life, length of, ch. 6 .. 460-461(v.41)

life, material, ch. 5 .. 329(intro.), df. 343(v.8,9)

Life of God, ch. 4 .. 308(v.35)

life on earth, ch. 5 .. 358(v.17); ch. 6 .. 461(v.41)

life, pure, ch. 5 .. 327(intro.)

life, purifier of, ch. 4 .. 311-312(v.38)

life, purpose of, ch. 6 .. 427(v.23)

life, spiritual, ch. 2 .. 87(v.8), 153(v.55), 156(v.57); ch. 3 .. 214
        (v.20); ch. 5 .. 359(v.18); ch. 6 .. 395(v.5)

life-supporting influence (see also positive influence), ch. 3 .. 198
        (v.11), 200-202(v.12-13), 204(v.14), 214(v.20); ch. 4 ..

276(v.17), 289(v.23), 309(v.36); ch. 5 .. 345(v.10); ch. 6 .. 439(v.28)

life, two ways of (see also householder, recluse), ch. 3 .. 184-186 (v.3); ch. 5 .. 335(v.5); ch. 6 .. 384-385(intro.-v.1)

life, wisdom of, ch. 1 .. 49-52(v.28)

life, withdrawal from, ch. 6 .. 405(v.10)

Lila-Shakti (power of the Absolute), ch. 4 .. 261(v.6)

limitations of individuality, ch. 3 .. 234(v.35); ch. 5 .. 350(v.13)

limitations of thought, speech and action, ch. 2 .. 146(v.52)

link between doer, action and its fruits, ch. 5 .. 351-353(v.14)

living for others (see also concern for others), ch. 1 .. 57-58 (v.33); ch. 2 .. 84(v.7), 111(v.34); ch. 3 .. 214-215(v.21), 217(v.24); ch. 5 .. 373-374(v.25)

living silence of Unity, ch. 6 .. 391-392(v.3)

logic, ch. 2 .. 103-104(v.26)

longevity, greatest, ch. 4 .. 253(v.1)

longing (see also craving), ch. 3 .. 225(v.30); ch. 4 .. 271(v.14)

longing, free from, ch. 2 .. 154-155(v.56); ch. 3 .. 225(v.30)

Lord: author of actions, ch. 3 .. 226(v.30)

Lord of all beings, ch. 4 .. 260-261(v.6); ch. 6 .. 467(v.47)

Lord of all the world, ch. 5 .. 379-380(v.29)

Lord of creation, ch. 2 .. 162(v.61); ch. 3 .. 196(v.10), 216(v.22), 225-226(v.30), 228(v.32); ch. 6 .. 411(v.14), 414(v.15), 446(v.31)

Lord of the yogis, ch. 5 .. 328(intro.)

Lord Shiva, ch. 4 .. 253(v.1)

Lord Vishnu, ch. 4 .. 253(v.1)

Lord's Being, ch. 4 .. 260(v.5), 265(v.9); ch. 6 .. 414(v.15)

loss, ch. 5 .. 327(intro.), 332(v.2)

loss and gain, ch. 2 .. 114-115(v.38), 139(v.49); ch. 5 .. 332(v.2)

loss during meditation, ch. 6 .. 404(v.10)

loss of the path, ch. 3 .. 232(v.35); ch. 5 .. 360(v.18)

loss of the Self, ch. 3 .. 213(v.20)

loss of *Yoga,* ch. 4 .. 255-256(v.2)

love (see also heart), ch. 1 .. 47-49(v.25-28), 53-54(v.30), 58 (v.34), 71(v.47); ch. 2 .. 76-77(v.1), 80-81(v.3), 127(v.45), 150(v.55), 157(v.57), 162(v.61); ch. 3 .. 216(v.22), 240 (v.39); ch. 4 .. 260(v.5), 264(v.8), 288(v.22), 293(v.25), 307(v.35), 315(v.38); ch. 5 .. 380(v.29); ch. 6 .. 443-444 (v.30), 459(v.39)

love and duty (see also heart and mind), ch. 1 .. 49-53(v.28-29), 53-54(v.30), 60-61(v.36), 71(v.47); ch. 2 .. 76(v.1)

love of God (see also devotion), ch. 4 .. 307(v.35)

love, universal, ch. 3 .. 214(v.20); ch. 4 .. 307(v.35)

lowest in human life, ch. 5 .. 360(v.18)

machinery that gives rise to desire, ch. 3 .. 240-241(v.39-40)

Madhava (Lord of fortune and slayer of the demon *Madha*), ch. 1 .. 37(v.14)

Mahabharata (the most authentic record of Indian history), ch. 4 .. 254(v.1)

'*mahat tattva*' (principle of intellect), ch. 6 .. 424(v.21)

man, ch. 4 .. df. 279(v.18)

man and God, difference between, ch. 4 .. 259(v.5)

man and God, relationship of, ch. 6 .. 443-450(v.30-32)

man, enlightened (see also integrated man, realized man), ch. 3 .. 224(v.29), 229-230(v.33); ch. 4 .. 291(v.24), 304(v.34)

man, great, ch. 1 .. 56-57(v.32-33), 65(v.40); ch. 3 .. 214-215 (v.21)

man, incarnation of, ch. 4 .. 259(v.5)

man, integrated (see also *jivan-mukti*, realized man), ch. 2 .. 86 (v.7), 135(v.48), 164(v.64); ch. 3 .. 211(v.19); ch. 4 .. 252(v.1)

man of action, ch. 3 .. 184(v.3); ch. 6 .. 465-466(v.46)

man of endeavor, ch. 6 .. 454(v.36)

man of knowledge, ch. 6 .. 465-466(v.46)

man of renunciation (see also *sanyasi*), ch. 5 .. 333-334(v.3)

man of thought, ch. 3 .. 184(v.3); ch. 6 .. 389-393(v.3)

man, undisciplined, ch. 6 .. 454-455(v.36)

man, wise (see also great man, realized man), ch. 3 .. 217-220 (v.25-26); ch. 5 .. 359(v.18)

manas (mind), ch. 6 .. 422(v.19)

manifest, ch. 2 .. 105-106(v.28-29); ch. 3 .. 213(v.20), 216(v.23), 220(v.27); ch. 4 .. 269(v.13); ch. 6 .. 468(v.47)

manifest creation, essential constituent of, ch. 3 .. 220(v.27)

manifestation, ch. 2 .. 141(v.49); ch. 3 .. 206(v.15), 216(v.23), 236(v.37); ch. 4 .. 261(v.6); ch. 6 .. 424(v.21)

manifestation, divine, ch. 4 .. 261-262(v.6-7)

manifestation, first, ch. 3 .. 206(v.15)

manifestation of *Brahman*, ch. 4 .. 262(v.7)

manifestation, purpose of, ch. 3 .. 236(v.37)

manifestation, second, ch. 3 .. 206(v.15)

man's link with God, ch. 3 .. 196(v.10)

mantra (see also medium of meditation), ch. 3 .. 198(v.11)

Manu, ch. 4 .. 254(v.1)

Manu (law-giver to the world), ch. 4 .. 252(v.1)

Manvantara, ch. 4 .. 254(v.1)

master, ch. 1 .. df. 29(v.2); ch. 2 .. 86(v.7), 89-90(v.10-11), 104
     (v.26); ch. 4 .. 257-259(v.2-4), 304-305(v.34); ch. 6 .. 459
     (v.39)

master, desire of the, ch. 4 .. 304(v.34)

master, mind of the, ch. 4 .. 304(v.34)

master, pleasing the, ch. 4 .. 304-305(v.34)

master-pupil relationship (see also teaching), ch. 2 .. 85-86(v.7),
     89-91(v.10-11), 104(v.26); ch. 3 .. 178-179(v.1), 182(v.2);
     ch. 4 .. 258-259(v.3-4), 261(v.6), 303-305(v.34); ch. 5 ..
     330(v.1); ch. 6 .. 459(v.39)

mastery of the higher Self, ch. 5 .. 339-341(v.7)

mastery of the lower self, ch. 5 .. 340(v.7)

mastery of the senses, ch. 2 .. 160(v.59); ch. 5 .. 340-341(v.7)

mastery over action, ch. 4 .. 291(v.24)

material life, ch. 5 .. 329(intro.), df. 343(v.8,9)

material means, *yagya* of, ch. 4 .. 302-303(v.33)

material prosperity, ch. 3 .. 200(v.12)

mature state of Union, ch. 4 .. 321(v.42)

means of gaining transcendental consciousness, ch. 3 .. 198(v.11)

means to attain God-consciousness, ch. 3 .. 211(v.19)

mechanics of bondage, ch. 3 .. 239(v.39); ch. 5 .. 349(v.12)

mechanics of evolution, ch. 1 .. 27(v.1)

mechanics of liberation, ch. 4 .. 285-287(v.20-21)

mechanics of maintaining two states of consciousness simulta-
     neously, ch. 3 .. 226(v.30); ch. 4 .. 314-315(v.38); ch. 5 ..
     362-363(v.20)

mechanics of nature (see also balancing force of nature, *dharma*),
     ch. 1 .. 43(v.21), 63(v.39)

mechanics of the influence of action, ch. 3 .. 197-198(v.11)

meditation (see also practice, technique, transcendental medita-
     tion), ch. 3 .. 183-186(v.3), 192-193(v.8), 213-214(v.20),
     219(v.26), 229(v.33); ch. 4 .. 263(v.8), 267(v.11), 282
     (v.19), 288-289(v.22-23), 292(v.24), 297(v.28), 301(v.32),

313(v.38), 317(v.39), 319(v.40); ch. 5 .. 326(intro.), 338
    (v.7), 356-357(v.17), 363(v.20), 375(v.26); ch. 6 .. 389-
    390(v.2-3), 393-394(v.4), 396-397(v.5), 402-417(v.10-17),
    421(v.19), 433-438(v.25-27), 444-445(v.30), 459-460(v.40-
    41), 462-463(v.43-44)

meditation and activity, ch. 3 .. 184-186(v.3), 194(v.9), 213(v.20),
    218-220(v.26), 226(v.30), 229(v.33); ch. 4 .. 292(v.24),
    312-314(v.38), 317(v.39), 320-322(v.41-42); ch. 5 .. 326
    (intro.), 335(v.4), 337(v.6), 344(v.10), 347-348(v.11);
    ch. 6 .. 386(v.1), 391(v.3), 402(v.10), 436(v.26)

meditation, discrimination in, ch. 6 .. 433(v.25)

meditation, disturbance during, ch. 6 .. 403(v.10)

meditation, evening, ch. 4 .. 313(v.38); ch. 5 .. 344(v.10), 357
    (v.17)

meditation, five conditions for, ch. 6 .. 402-405(v.10)

meditation, inward stroke of, ch. 3 .. 193(v.8), 214(v.20), 225
    (v.30); ch. 4 .. 313(v.38); ch. 5 .. 340(v.7), 344(v.10);
    ch. 6 .. 409-411(v.14), 428(v.23), 430-431(v.24), 434-436
    (v.25-26), 438(v.27)

meditation, loss during, ch. 6 .. 404(v.10)

meditation, medium of (see also *mantra*), ch. 4 .. 301(v.32); ch.
    6 .. 407(v.12), 421-422(v.19), 435(v.26), 437(v.27)

meditation, morning, ch. 4 .. 313(v.38); ch. 5 .. 344(v.10), 357
    (v.17)

meditation, outward stroke of, ch. 3 .. 193(v.8); ch. 5 .. 340(v.7),
    344(v.10); ch. 6 .. 431(v.24), 435-436(v.26), 438(v.27)

meditation, place of, ch. 6 .. 405-406(v.11)

meditation, position for, ch. 6 .. 406-409(v.12-13)

meditation, thoughts in, ch. 6 .. 411(v.14)

medium of meditation (see also *mantra*), ch. 4 .. 301(v.32); ch.
    6 .. 407(v.12), 421-422(v.19), 435(v.26), 437(v.27)

memory, ch. 2 .. 163-164(v.63)

mental activity (see also thinking), ch. 3 .. 184(v.3), 189(v.6);
    ch. 4 .. 302(v.33), 315(v.38), 322(v.42); ch. 5 .. 326
    (intro.), 335(v.4), 348(v.11), 369(v.23); ch. 6 .. 394(v.4),
    434(v.25)

mental and physical aspects, culture of, ch. 5 .. 369(v.23)

mental process, ch. 6 .. 430-431(v.24)

metabolism, ch. 2 .. 166(v.66), 173(v.72); ch. 3 .. 221(v.27);
    ch. 4 .. 298-299(v.30), 313(v.38); ch. 5 .. 346(v.11)

metaphysics of Union with God, ch. 6 .. 449(v.32)

milk of the *Upanishads,* ch. 6 .. 443(v.29)

mind (see also conscious mind), ch. 1 .. 49-53(v.28-29), 53-54
    (v.30), 60-61(v.36), 71(v.47); ch. 2 .. 76-77(v.1), 98(v.18),
    117-127(v.39-45), 136-144(v.48-51), 150-157(v.55-57), 160-
    162(v.59-61), 164-169(v.64-68), 171-174(v.71-72); ch. 3 ..
    179(v.1), 183-185(v.3), 187(v.4), 189-190(v.6-7), 193(v.8),
    195(v.9), 202-205(v.13-14), 207(v.16), 210-211(v.19), 213-
    214(v.20), 218-219(v.26), 221(v.27), 223-224(v.28-29),
    226(v.30), 230-231(v.33-34), 237(v.37), 240-244(v.39-43);
    ch. 4 .. 263(v.8), 266(v.10), 276(v.17), 278(v.18), 282-291
    (v.19-24), 293(v.25), 295-296(v.27), 298-301(v.29-32), 295-
    296(v.27), 303-304(v.34), 311-314(v.37-38), 316-318(v.39),
    320(v.41), 322(v.42); ch. 5 .. 328(intro.), 330(v.1), 332-
    333(v.2-3), 337-348(v.6-11), 350(v.13), 357-362(v.17-20),
    364(v.21), 366(v.22), 368-372(v.23-24), 374-376(v.25-26),
    377-378(v.28); ch. 6 .. 386-387(v.1), 389-391(v.2-3), 393-
    413(v.4-15), 415-416(v.16-17), 418-425(v.18-21), 428-438
    (v.23-27), 440(v.28), 442(v.29), 444-445(v.30-31), 450-456
    (v.33-37), 460(v.41), 466-467(v.46-47)
mind and body, coordination of, ch. 1 .. 53(v.29); ch. 2 .. 123
    (v.42); ch. 5 .. 340(v.7)
mind and body subdued, ch. 6 .. 402-405(v.10)
mind and desires, ch. 3 .. 243(v.43)
mind and heart (see heart and mind)
mind and nervous system, relationship of, ch. 6 .. 390(v.3)
mind and senses, coordination of, ch. 2 .. 87(v.8); ch. 5 .. 340-
    341(v.7)
mind, balance of, ch. 2 .. 135-141(v.48-49), 154(v.56), 164
    (v.63); ch. 6 .. 400(v.8)
mind: channeling in one direction (see also convergence, one-
    pointed), ch. 2 .. 121(v.41); ch. 6 .. 435-436(v.26), 452
    (v.35)
mind, coarse, ch. 3 .. 207(v.15)
mind, control of the, ch. 4 .. 295(v.27); ch. 6 .. 452-453(v.35)
mind, cosmic, ch. 2 .. 136-137(v.48); ch. 4 .. 304(v.34); ch. 6 ..
    397(v.6), 464(v.45)
mind, desires of the, ch. 2 .. 151(v.55)
mind, disciplined, ch. 6 .. 412-413(v.15), 439(v.28), 454-455(v.36)
mind, dividing the, ch. 3 .. 185(v.3, 218-219(v.26)
mind, doubting (see also doubt), ch. 4 .. 318-319(v.40)
mind, essential nature of, ch. 2 .. 78(v.2)
mind, evenness of (see also balance of mind, steady intellect), ch.
    2 .. 94-95(v.15), 121(v.41), 164(v.64); ch. 4 .. 288(v.22);
    ch. 5 .. 361(v.19); ch. 6 .. 401(v.9), 451(v.34)

mind, individual, ch. 6 .. 437(v.27)

mind, irresolute, ch. 2 .. 121-125(v.41-44)

mind, movement of the, ch. 2 .. 118-119(v.40), 121(v.41), 136 (v.48); ch. 3 .. 238-240(v.39); ch. 6 .. 440(v.28)

mind, natural tendency of the, ch. 2 .. 118-120(v.40), 167-169 (v.67-68); ch. 3 .. 210(v.19), 229(v.33), 239(v.39); ch. 4 .. 267(v.11); ch. 5 .. 332-333(v.2), 337(v.6); ch. 6 .. 404-405(v.10), 411(v.14), 432(v.25), 436(v.26), 452(v.35), 455(v.36)

mind of the master, ch. 4 .. 304(v.34)

mind, principle of, ch. 6 .. 424(v.21)

mind, purified state of, ch. 6 .. 460(v.41)

mind, quality of, ch. 3 .. 203(v.13)

mind, sorrow in, ch. 2 .. 155(v.56)

mind, stages of, ch. 2 .. 166(v.66)

mind, steadiness of (see also steady intellect), ch. 2 .. 166-167 (v.66); ch. 6 .. 390(v.3), 452-453(v.35)

mind, wandering, ch. 2 .. 117-121(v.39-41), 160(v.59), 166(v.66); ch. 5 .. 371(v.24); ch. 6 .. 413(v.15), 451-453(v.34-35)

mind, wavering, ch. 6 .. 435-436(v.26), 450-453(v.33-35)

mind, weakness of, ch. 2 .. 78(v.2); ch. 6 .. 436(v.26)

misfortune, ch. 6 .. 459(v.40)

misfortune of others, ch. 1 .. 72(v.47)

misinterpretations (see misunderstandings)

misunderstandings, ch. 2 .. 94(v.15), 114(v.38), 124-125(v.43-44), 134-136(v.47-48), 139-140(v.49), 142(v.50), 151-153(v.55), 156-157(v.57), 160(v.59), 171(v.70); ch. 3 .. 184(v.3), 199(v.12), 209(v.18), 219(v.26), 224(v.29), 231(v.34), 239 (v.39), 241(v.41), 244(v.43); ch. 4 .. 254(v.1), 257(v.2), 266(v.10), 285(v.19), 294-295(v.26-27); ch. 5 .. 330(v.1), 345(v.10), 365(v.21), 370(v.23); ch. 6 .. 386-387(v.1), 405 (v.10), 408(v.13), 433-435(v.25-26), 442(v.29), 446(v.31), 450-452(v.33-34), 464(v.45)

moderation, ch. 6 .. 414-418(v.16-17)

moksha (liberation), ch. 6 .. 427-428(v.23)

mood-making, ch. 2 .. 94(v.15), 114(v.38), 135(v.48), 139(v.49), 152(v.55), 156(v.57); ch. 3 .. 199(v.12), 226(v.30); ch. 4 .. 290(v.24); ch. 5 .. 342(v.8,9), 345(v.10), 365(v.21); ch. 6 .. 386-387(v.1), 411(v.14), 442(v.29)

moral code (see also values), ch. 2 .. 110(v.33)

morality, virtue and right action, basis of, ch. 6 .. 427(v.23)

morning meditation (see also meditation, transcendental meditation), ch. 4 .. 313(v.38); ch. 5 .. 344(v.10), 357(v.17)

Mother Divine, ch. 4 .. 253(v.1)

motion, ch. 3 .. 236(v.37)

movement of the mind, ch. 2 .. 118-119(v.40), 121 (v.41), 136 (v.48); ch. 3 .. 238-240(v.39); ch. 6 .. 440(v.28)

multiplicity (see also diversity), ch. 2 .. 96(v.16), 126(v.45); ch. 5 .. 340(v.7); ch. 6 .. 423(v.20), 445(v.30)

muni (sage), ch. 2 .. 154-155(v.56), 169-170(v.69); ch. 5 .. 377 (v.28); ch. 6 .. 389-390(v.3), df. 389(v.3)

mystical experience, ch. 6 .. 444-445(v.30)

naishkarmyam (non-action), ch. 3 .. 187(v.4)

natural action, ch. 3 .. 210-212(v.19), 229-230(v.33); ch. 5 .. 352(v.14)

natural behaviour, ch. 3 .. 209(v.18)

natural duty (see also allotted duty), ch. 2 .. 108(v.31), 113 (v.37); ch. 3 .. 191-193(v.8)

natural duty, criterion of, ch. 3 .. 192(v.8)

natural pattern of existence, ch. 2 .. 133(v.46)

natural seat of bondage, ch. 3 .. 230-231 (v.33-34)

natural tendency of the mind, ch. 2 .. 118-120(v.40), 167-169 (v.67-68); ch. 3 .. 210(v.19), 229(v.33), 239(v.39); ch. 4 .. 267(v.11); ch. 5 .. 332-333(v.2), 337(v.6); ch. 6 .. 404-405(v.10), 411(v.14), 432(v.25), 436(v.26), 452(v.35), 455(v.36)

natural tendency of the senses, ch. 6 .. 431(v.24)

Nature, ch. 1 .. 35(v.13), 42(v.20); ch. 2 .. 128(v.45); ch. 3 .. 188(v.5), 206(v.15), 220(v.27), 224(v.29), 233(v.35); ch. 4 .. 256(v.2), 284(v.19), 309(v.36); ch. 5 .. 345(v.10), 351-353(v.14), 379(v.29); ch. 6 .. 424(v.21)

nature, basis of, ch. 4 .. 284(v.19)

nature, command of, ch. 5 .. 360-361(v.19)

nature, laws of (see also cosmic law), ch. 1 .. 63(v.39); ch. 2 .. 123(v.42), 133(v.46); ch. 3 .. 191-192(v.8), 195(v.9), 197-198(v.11), 205(v.14), 242(v.41); ch. 4 .. 276-277(v.17), 284(v.19), 308(v.36); ch. 6 .. 392(v.3), 416-417(v.17), 427(v.23), 430-431(v.24), 438-439(v.27-28)

nature, mechanics of (see also balancing force of nature, *dharma*), ch. 1 .. 43(v.21), 63(v.39)

nature, needs of, ch. 4 .. 287(v.22)

nature of action, ch. 4 .. 250(intro.); ch. 5 .. 330(v.1)

nature of *Brahman,* ch. 6 .. 440-442(v.28-29)

nature of *Krishna,* ch. 4 .. 260-261(v.6), 272-273(v.14-15)

nature of the Absolute, ch. 3 .. 188(v.5)

nature of the actor, ch. 4 .. 250(intro.)

nature, response of, ch. 3 .. 199(v.12)

nature, support of, ch. 2 .. 133(v.46); ch. 3 .. 197(v.11), 233-234(v.35); ch. 5 .. 350(v.13), 375(v.26); ch. 6 .. 463(v.44)

need for action, ch. 2 .. 114(v.38); ch. 4 .. 268(v.12)

need to learn, ch. 1 .. 47(v.25)

needs of nature, ch. 4 .. 287(v.22)

negative forces, ch. 1 .. 27(v.1), 38(v.15), 54(v.30); ch. 2 .. 108 (v.31); ch. 4 .. 264(v.8)

negative influence (see also life-damaging influence), ch. 1 .. 60 (v.36); ch. 2 .. 143(v.50); ch. 3 .. 227(v.31)

nervous system, ch. 2 .. 96(v.17), 166(v.66), 168(v.68), 173 (v.72); ch. 3 .. df. 226(v.30), 234(v.35); ch. 4 .. 298(v.29), 309(v.36), 313-315(v.38); ch. 5 .. 346(v.11), 369(v.23); ch. 6 .. 390(v.3), 393(v.3), 403(v.10), 407(v.12), 416 (v.17), 429-431(v.24), 436(v.26), 439-440(v.28)

nervous system and mind, relationship of, ch. 6 .. 390(v.3)

nervous system, coarseness in the, ch. 4 .. 309(v.36)

nervous system, culture of the, ch. 4 .. 314-315(v.38); ch. 6 .. 431(v.24)

nervous system, integration of functions of the, ch. 4 .. 315(v.38)

nervous system, normalization of the, ch. 6 .. 407(v.12)

nervous system, purity of the, ch. 6 .. 439-440(v.28)

nervous system, refinement of, ch. 6 .. 439-440(v.28), 466(v.46)

nervous system, two levels of function in the, ch. 4 .. 314-315(v.38)

nirvikalpa samadhi (cosmic consciousness), ch. 4 .. 317(v.39)

niryogakshema ("independent of possessions"), ch. 2 .. 130(v.45)

nistraigunyo bhav Arjuna (Be without the three gunas, Arjuna), ch. 2 .. 138(v.49)

nitya-samadhi (cosmic consciousness), ch. 2 .. 150-151(v.55); ch. 6 .. 402(v.10)

niyama (organized), ch. 3 .. 241(v.41); ch. 6 .. 435(v.26)

no activity (see also inactivity), ch. 3 .. 188(v.5); ch. 6 .. 437 (v.27)

no destruction, ch. 6 .. 459(v.40)

non-action (see non-attachment), ch. 3 .. 186-188(v.4-5), 230 (v.33); ch. 6 .. 393(v.3)

non-anticipation, ch. 2 .. 134(v.47)

non-attachment (see also detachment), ch. 2 .. 138-145(v.49-51), 156-159(v.57-58); ch. 3 .. 187(v.4), 218(v.25), 229-230 (v.33); ch. 4 .. 250(intro.), 282-283(v.19), 285(v.19-20), 307(v.35); ch. 5 .. 330(v.1), 337(v.6), 342(v.8,9), 347 (v.11), 352(v.14), 378(v.28); ch. 6 .. 386(v.1), 411(v.14), 434(v.25), 452-454(v.35-36)

non-attachment, thinking of, ch. 6 .. 386-387(v.1)

non-doer (see also separation of Self and activity), ch. 3 .. 225 (v.30); ch. 4 .. 269-270(v.13); ch. 5 .. 379(v.29)

non-indulgence of the senses, ch. 2 .. 159(v.58)

non-involvement of the Supreme, ch. 4 .. 272(v.14), 275(v.16); ch. 5 .. 354(v.15)

normalization, ch. 6 .. 407(v.12), 416(v.17)

nose, front of his, ch. 6 .. 408(v.13)

obedience, ch. 4 .. 304(v.34)

object of attention, ch. 3 .. 223(v.28); ch. 6 .. 436(v.26)

object of experience, ch. 3 .. 230-231(v.33-34); ch. 5 .. 343-344 (v.8,9); ch. 6 .. 421-422(v.19), 468(v.47)

objective, ch. 2 .. 154(v.56); ch. 3 .. 222(v.28); ch. 5 .. 352(v.14); ch. 6 .. 421(v.19), 425(v.21)

objective experience, ch. 6 .. 398(v.6), 421(v.19)

objects of the senses, ch. 2 .. 158-161(v.58-60), 163-164(v.62-64), 167-169(v.67-68); ch. 3 .. 189-190(v.6-7), 230-231(v.34), 236(v.37); ch. 4 .. 264(v.8), 266(v.10), 293-294(v.26), 298 (v.30); ch. 5 .. 342-343(v.8,9), 362(v.20), 364-368 (v.21-22), 377(v.27); ch. 6 .. 393-394(v.4), 396(v.5), 407(v.12), 414-415(v.16), 420-422(v.18-19), 455(v.36)

obstacle, ch. 2 .. 117-120(v.40), 163(v.62); ch. 4 .. 309(v.36); ch. 6 .. 456(v.37)

obstruction of desire, ch. 3 .. 236-237(v.37)

offering, ch. 4 .. 290(v.24), 302(v.33)

offering to the gods, ch. 3 .. 198-199(v.11-12); ch. 4 .. 268(v.12), 292-293(v.25)

omens, ch. 1 .. 55(v.31)

one-pointed (see also convergence), ch. 2 .. 121(v.41), 125-126 (v.44-45), 131(v.45), 139(v.49); ch. 4 .. 294(v.26); ch. 6 .. 406(v.12), 408(v.13), 463(v.44)

oneness (see also Unity), ch. 3 .. 211-212(v.19), 240(v.39); ch. 4 .. 266(v.10), 290(v.24), 305(v.35), 308(v.36), 310(v.37); ch. 5 .. 347(v.11), 358-361(v.17-19); ch. 6 .. 392(v.3), 426 (v.22), 443(v.30), 445(v.30), 448-449(v.32), 450-451(v.33), 468(v.47)

opposites (see also extremes), ch. 4 .. 287-288(v.22); ch. 5 .. 333-334(v.3); ch. 6 .. 448(v.32)

order, fourfold, ch. 4 .. 269-270(v.13); ch. 5 .. 379(v.29)

order, social, ch. 1 .. 66-67(v.42), 70(v.45); ch. 2 .. 110(v.33); ch. 3 .. 191(v.8)

organized senses, ch. 3 .. 190(v.7), 241-243(v.41-42)

organs of action, ch. 3 .. 189-190(v.6-7); ch. 4 .. 286(v.20), 315 (v.38); ch. 6 .. 429(v.24)

organs of action, restraining the, ch. 3 .. 189(v.6)

origin of action, ch. 2 .. 140(v.49)

origin of the senses, ch. 6 .. 424-425(v.21)

others, concern for (see also living for others), ch. 1 .. 52(v.29), 56-57(v.32-33), 72(v.47); ch. 2 .. 83(v.6)

others, die for, ch. 2 .. 111(v.34)

others, living for (see also concern for others), ch. 1 .. 57-58 (v.33); ch. 2 .. 84(v.7), 111(v.34); ch. 3 .. 214-215(v.21), 217(v.24); ch. 5 .. 373-374(v.25)

others, misfortune of, ch. 1 .. 72(v.47)

others, relationship with, ch. 2 .. 115(v.38)

others, speaking ill of, ch. 3 .. 227(v.31)

outer experience (see also experience), ch. 2 .. 158(v.58); ch. 5 .. 328(intro.), 364(v.21), 371-372(v.24), 376-377(v.27); ch. 6 .. 393(v.4)

outer stimulus, ch. 3 .. 238(v.38)

outward activity, ch. 3 .. 213(v.20); ch. 4 .. 292(v.24)

outward sign, ch. 2 .. 149(v.54), 153(v.55), 158(v.58), 173(v.72)

outward stroke of meditation, ch. 3 .. 193(v.8); ch. 5 .. 340(v.7), 344(v.10); ch. 6 .. 431(v.24), 435-436(v.26), 438(v.27)

overshadow, ch. 3 .. 202(v.13), 237-238(v.37-38), 240-242(v.40-41); ch. 4 .. 257(v.2), 263(v.7), 278(v.18), 303(v.34); ch. 5 .. 338-339(v.7), 343-344(v.8,9), 372(v.24); ch. 6 .. 387 (v.1), 419(v.18), 438(v.27), 467(v.47)

pain, ch. 2 .. 93-95(v.14-15), 112(v.36); ch. 6 .. 447(v.32)

passivity, ch. 6 .. 415(v.16)

past, ch. 4 .. 252-259(v.1-4), 285(v.20), 311(v.37); ch. 6 .. 463 (v.44)

past actions, influence of (see also action-reaction, *karma*), ch. 4 ..
     259(v.5), 311(v.37)

past and present, ch. 4 .. 252(v.1), 259(v.4), 311(v.37)

path, loss of the, ch. 3 .. 232(v.35); ch. 5 .. 360(v.18)

path of liberation from bondage, ch. 3 .. 222(v.28)

path to *Brahman,* ch. 6 .. 457-458(v.38)

pathless path, ch. 2 .. 119(v.40)

patience, ch. 6 .. 432-434(v.25)

peace (see also contentment), ch. 2 .. 165-167(v.66), 170-172
     (v.70-71); ch. 4 .. 316(v.39), 318(v.39); ch. 5 .. 348-349
     (v.12), 379-380(v.29); ch. 6 .. 399(v.7), 409(v.14), 412-
     416(v.15-17), 424(v.20), 437-439(v.27-28)

people, two types of, ch. 3 .. 184-186(v.3); ch. 4 .. 294(v.26);
     ch. 5 .. 335(v.5)

perception, ch. 6 .. 443(v.30)

perception, senses of, ch. 3 .. 190(v.7); ch. 5 .. 341(v.7); ch. 6 ..
     429(v.24)

perfect detachment, ch. 5 .. 334(v.3)

perfect liberation, ch. 6 .. 448(v.32)

perfect renunciation, ch. 5 .. 327(intro.), 332(v.2), 351(v.14),
     378(v.28)

perfection, ch. 3 .. 186-188(v.4), 196-197(v.9-11), 212-213(v.20),
     215(v.22); ch. 4 .. 280(v.18), 312(v.38); ch. 5 .. 327
     (intro.); ch. 6 .. 395(v.5), 462(v.43), 464(v.45)

perform, ability to, ch. 3 .. 231-234(v.35)

performance of action, ch. 2 .. 118(v.40), 143(v.50); ch. 5 ..
     327(intro.), 330(v.1), 346-348(v.11)

perishable, ch. 2 .. 115(v.38), 128(v.45); ch. 3 .. 179-180(v.1);
     ch. 5 .. 334(v.4); ch. 6 .. 449(v.32)

personal God, ch. 6 .. 444-450(v.30-32)

phenomena, ch. 2 .. 79(v.2), 93(v.14), 104(v.27), 108(v.31);
     ch. 6 .. 449(v.32)

philosopher-kings, ch. 4 .. 255(v.2)

philosophy of action, ch. 5 .. 327-328(intro.)

philosophy of renunciation, ch. 5 .. 327-328(intro.), 373(v.25),
     378(v.28)

philosophy of the integrated life, ch. 5 .. 328(intro.)

physical activity, ch. 5 .. 369(v.23)

physics, ch. 2 .. 105(v.28)

physiological, ch. 3 .. 221(v.27)

physiology of gaining cosmic consciousness, ch. 4 .. 314(v.38)

physiology of gaining God-consciousness, ch. 4 .. 315(v.38)

Pindodaka, ch. 1 .. df. 66-67(v.42)

pious (see also righteousness, virtue), ch. 3 .. 203(v.13)

pitiable, ch. 2 .. 140(v.49)

place of meditation, ch. 6 .. 405-406(v.11)

planes of existence, ch. 6 .. 460-461(v.41)

play with God, ch. 6 .. 449(v.32)

playground for the Divine, ch. 4 .. 250(intro.), 260(v.5)

pleasing the gods, ch. 3 .. 194(v.9), 198-199(v.11-12)

pleasing the master, ch. 4 .. 304-305(v.34)

pleasure (see also enjoyment, happpiness), ch. 2 .. 93-95(v.14-15); ch. 5 .. 366-368(v.22); ch. 6 .. 418-420(v.18), 447-449(v.32)

pleasure and pain, ch. 2 .. 93-95(v.14-15), 154-156(v.56-57); ch. 4 .. 288(v.22); ch. 6 .. 399(v.7), 447-448(v.32)

position for meditation, ch. 6 .. 406-409(v.12-13)

positive forces, ch. 1 .. 27(v.1), 38(v.15); ch. 2 .. 108(v.31)

positive influence (see also life-supporting influence), ch. 2 .. 143 (v.50)

possessed of the Self, ch. 4 .. 319-321(v.41)

possessions, ch. 4 .. 297(v.28); ch. 6 .. 402-405(v.10)

possessions, independent of, ch. 2 .. 126-132(v.45); ch. 4 .. 286-287(v.21)

possessions, without, ch. 6 .. 402-405(v.10)

power, ch. 3 .. 244(v.43); ch. 4 .. 262-263(v.7), 300(v.31); ch. 5 .. 361(v.19), 367(v.22); ch. 6 .. 414(v.15)

power of creation, *Krishna's,* ch. 4 .. 260-261(v.6)

power of the Absolute, ch. 4 .. 261(v.6)

power of the Almighty, ch. 3 .. 225-226(v.30); ch. 4 .. 263(v.7)

powerful thought, ch. 3 .. 214(v.20)

practical, ch. 2 .. 84(v.7), 113(v.37), 120(v.40), 123(v.42), 127 (v.45), 149(v.54), 150(v.55); ch. 3 .. 177-178(intro.), 182-183(v.2), 185(v.3), 199(v.12), 211(v.19), 219(v.26), 224 (v.29), 235(v.36), 239(v.39), 244(v.43); ch. 4 .. 278(v.17), 280-281(v.18), 290(v.23), 313(v.38), 320-321(v.41-42); ch. 5 .. 328(intro.), 330(v.1), 344(v.10), 356(v.16); ch. 6 .. 384(intro.), 397(v.6), 419(v.18), 442(v.29), 446-447(v.31-32), 453(v.35), 456-457(v.37)

practice (see also technique, transcendental meditation), ch. 2 .. 116-120(v.39-40), 126(v.45); ch. 3 .. 186(v.3), 201(v.13),

214(v.20), 227-228(v.31-32); ch. 4 .. 249-250(intro.), 255-256(v.2), 297-298(v.28-29), 300-301(v.31-32), 306(v.35), 312(v.38), 315(v.38), 317(v.39), 319-321(v.40-42); ch. 5 .. 328(intro.), 331(v.2), 334-335(v.3-4), 337-338(v.6-7), 340(v.7), 345(v.10-11), 365(v.21), 370(v.23), 376-378 (v.26-28); ch. 6 .. 384-385(v.1), 389-390(v.2-3), 396-397 (v.5-6), 401-402(v.9-10), 405(v.10), 407(v.12), 412(v.15), 417-418(v.17-18), 423(v.20), 427(v.23), 429-431(v.24), 434(v.25), 440(v.28), 444(v.30), 452-454(v.34-36), 457-466(v.38-46)

practice, former, ch. 6 .. 463(v.44)

practice, lack of, ch. 6 .. 465(v.45)

practising renunciation, ch. 5 .. 326(intro.)

Pragya (intellect), ch. 2 .. 151(v.55)

"pragyanam brahma" ("wisdom is the Absolute"), ch. 5 .. 355 (v.16)

prakriti (Nature), ch. 2 .. 128(v.45); ch. 3 .. 188(v.5), 206(v.15), 220-222(v.27-28); ch. 4 .. 261(v.6), 307(v.35); ch. 6 .. 424 (v.21)

pratyavaya (obstacle), ch. 2 .. 117(v.40)

prayer, ch. 6 .. 447(v.31)

prerequisite of *Karma Yoga* and *Sanyasa,* ch. 6 .. 387(v.1)

prerequisite to freedom, ch. 3 .. 227(v.31)

prerequisite to knowledge, ch. 4 .. 316(v.39)

prerequisite to the realization of God, ch. 3 .. 227(v.31)

prerequisite to cosmic consciousness, ch. 6 .. 438(v.27)

prerequisites to success in *Yoga,* ch. 6 .. 454(v.36)

present and past, ch. 4 .. 252(v.1), 259(v.4)

principle of action, ch. 1 .. 69(v.44); ch. 6 .. 461(v.41)

principle of intellect, ch. 6 .. 424(v.21)

principle of mind, ch. 6 .. 424(v.21)

principle of the second element, ch. 2 .. 126(v.45)

problem, solution to any, ch. 3 .. 234(v.35)

problems, ch. 1 .. 52(v.28), 56(v.32), 58(v.34), 66(v.41); ch. 2 .. 78-71(v.2-3), 87(v.8), 146(v.52); ch. 3 .. 234(v.35)

process, mental, ch. 6 .. 430-431(v.24)

process of action, ch. 2 .. 134(v.47), 143(v.50); ch. 3 .. 191(v.8); ch. 4 .. 278(v.18), 281-283(v.19)

process of creation (see also creation), ch. 3 .. 206(v.15)

process of evolution (see also evolution), ch. 3 .. 188(v.5), 231 (v.35), 233(v.35)

process of experience (see also direct experience, experience), ch. 3 . . 206(v.15), 219(v.26); ch. 5 . . 365(v.21)

process of manifestation (see also manifestation), ch. 3 . . 206 (v.15), 236(v.37)

process of thinking (see also thinking), ch. 3 . . 219(v.26); ch. 6 . . 403-404(v.10), 406(v.12)

progress, continuity of, ch. 3 . . 233(v.35)

progress, sense of, ch. 2 . . 125(v.44)

progress, spiritual, ch. 3 . . 185(v.3)

proper means of gaining *Yoga,* ch. 6 . . 454-455(v.36)

proper sense of values, ch. 6 . . 453-454(v.35-36)

proper use of the senses, ch. 4 . . 294(v.26)

proportion, sense of, ch. 2 . . 130(v.45)

prosperity of the individual, ch. 3 . . 196(v.10), 199-200(v.12)

pure consciousness (see also transcendental consciousness), ch. 2 . . 129(v.45), 147-148(v.53), 152(v.55), 164(v.64); ch. 3 . . 190(v.7), 207(v.16), 214(v.20), 223(v.28), 228(v.32), 236 (v.37), 238(v.38); ch. 4 . . 277(v.17), 291(v.24), 294-295 (v.26-27), 302(v.33), 309-310(v.36-37); 312(v.38); ch. 5 . . 347(v.11), 361(v.19), 374(v.25); ch. 6 . . 394(v.4), 397 (v.6), 407(v.12), 412(v.14), 418-419(v.17-18), 437(v.27), 445(v.30)

pure life, ch. 5 . . 327(intro.)

pure of spirit, ch. 5 . . 338(v.7)

purification, ch. 4 . . 264(v.8), 265-266(v.10), 297-300(v.28-31), 302(v.33), 311-312(v.38); ch. 5 . . 345-348(v.11), 379(v.29); ch. 6 . . 390(v.3), 406-407(v.12), 464-466(v.45-46)

purified of all sin, ch. 6 . . 464(v.45)

purified state of mind, ch. 6 . . 460(v.41)

purifier of life, ch. 4 . . 311-312(v.38)

purity, ch. 1 . . 37(v.14), 66(v.41-42); ch. 2 . . 126-132(v.45), 146(v.52); ch. 4 . . 256(v.2), 263(v.8), 266(v.10), 300 (v.31), 312(v.38); ch. 5 . . 338-339(v.7), 356-358(v.17); ch. 6 . . 390(v.3), 395(v.5), 421(v.19), 423(v.20), 438-440(v.27-28), 444-445(v.30), 459-462(v.40-43), 464-466(v.45-46)

purity, least, ch. 6 . . 461(v.41)

purity of blood, ch. 1 . . 66(v.42)

purity of heart, ch. 1 . . 55(v.31)

purity of nervous system, ch. 6 . . 439-440(v.28)

purity of teaching, ch. 4 . . 255-257(v.2)

purnamadah purnamidam, ch. 2 .. df. 79(v.2); ch. 4 .. 250
    (intro.), 279(v.18); ch. 6 .. 449(v.32)

purpose, cosmic, ch. 3 .. 192(v.8), 202-204(v.13-14), 209(v.18);
    ch. 4 .. 251(v.1), 276(v.17), 287(v.22); ch. 5 .. 346(v.11);
    ch. 6 .. 439(v.28)

purpose of action, ch. 2 .. 114(v.38); ch. 3 .. 208-209(v.17-18),
    212(v.19); ch. 4 .. 283(v.19)

purpose of all activity, ch. 2 .. 132(v.45); ch. 3 .. 208-209(v.17-
    18), 212(v.19)

purpose of all possible desires, ch. 2 .. 170(v.70); ch. 3 .. 208-
    209(v.17-18)

purpose of creation, ch. 1 .. 62(v.37); ch. 2 .. 104(v.27); ch. 3 ..
    204(v.14), 236-237(v.37); ch. 5 .. 352(v.14), 380(v.29)

purpose of evolution, ch. 4 .. 291(v.24)

purpose of *Karma Yoga,* ch. 5 .. 332(v.2)

purpose of life, ch. 6 .. 427(v.23)

purpose of manifestation, ch. 3 .. 236(v.37)

purpose of recreation, ch. 6 .. 417(v.17)

purpose of *Yoga,* ch. 6 .. 428(v.23)

purpose, start and progress of action, ch. 4 .. 281-283(v.19)

quality of action, ch. 4 .. 283(v.19)

quality of experience, ch. 6 .. 442(v.29)

quality of food, ch. 3 .. 203(v.13)

quality of fruit of action, ch. 5 .. 351(v.14)

quality of silence, ch. 6 .. 392(v.3)

quality of the mind, ch. 3 .. 203(v.13)

question and answer, ch. 3 .. 179(v.1)

rain, ch. 3 .. 204-205(v.14)

rajas (maintaining *guna*), ch. 2 .. 128(v.45); ch. 3 .. 220(v.27),
    224(v.29), 236-237(v.37); ch. 4 .. 262(v.7), 269(v.13), 306
    (v.35); ch. 5 .. 359-360(v.18); ch. 6 .. 424(v.21), 437(v.27)

Reality, ch. 2 .. 79(v.2), 90(v.11), 93-96(v.14-17), 100-103(v.21-
    25), 106-107(v.29), 116(v.39), 120(v.40), 125(v.44), 136
    (v.48), 146-148(v.52-53), 152(v.55); ch. 3 .. 183(v.3), 195
    (v.9), 213(v.20), 224(v.28-29), 226(v.30), 244(v.43); ch.
    4 .. 251(intro.), 256(v.2), 277(v.17), 279(v.18), 291-292
    (v.24), 301-304(v.32-34), 318-320(v.39-41), 322(v.42); ch.
    5 .. 344(v.10), 354(v.15), 357-359(v.17-18), 361-363(v.19-
    20), 367(v.22), 375(v.26); ch. 6 .. 383(intro.), 400(v.8),
    438-439(v.27-28), 442(v.29), 449(v.32), 468(v.47)

Reality, intellectual conception of, ch. 2 .. 100(v.21), 103(v.25), 106-107(v.29); ch. 5 .. 363(v.20); ch. 6 .. 400(v.8)

realization (see also enlightenment), ch. 2 .. 120(v.40), 126 (v.45), 129(v.45), 132-133(v.46), 146-147(v.52-53), 153 (v.55); ch. 3 .. 184(v.3), 204(v.14), 219(v.26), 221(v.28), 225(v.30), 228(v.32), 230(v.33), 241-242(v.41), 244(v.43); ch. 4 .. 292(v.24), 313(v.38); ch. 5 .. 346(v.11), 353(v.14), 371(v.24), 378(v.28); ch. 6 .. 390(v.3)

realization, height of, ch. 6 .. 449(v.32)

realization of God (see also God-consciousness), ch. 3 .. 196 (v.10), 210(v.19), 227(v.31); ch. 4 .. 272(v.14); ch. 5 .. 380(v.29); ch. 6 .. 444(v.30), 452(v.34)

realization of God, prerequisite to, ch. 3 .. 227(v.31)

realization, two aspects of, ch. 6 .. 400(v.8)

realization, two conditions for, ch. 5 .. 363(v.20)

realized man, behaviour of, ch. 2 .. 155-157(v.56-57); ch. 3 .. 209(v.18); ch. 4 .. 290(v.23); ch. 6 .. 401(v.9)

realized man, characteristics of, ch. 2 .. 148-174(v.54-72); ch. 4 .. 278-292(v.18-24); ch. 5 .. 358-380(v.18-29); ch. 6 .. 397-401(v.6-9)

rebirth (see reincarnation)

receptivity, ch. 4 .. 303(v.34)

receptivity in transcendental meditation, ch. 6 .. 433(v.25)

recluse, ch. 2 .. 149(v.54), 151-153(v.55), 157(v.57); ch. 3 .. 183-186(v.3), 244-245(v.43); ch. 4 .. 249(intro.), 257(v.2); ch. 5 .. 326(intro.), 329(intro.), 335(v.5), 348(v.11); ch. 6 .. 384-385(intro.-v.1), 388(v.2), 396(v.5)

recreation, ch. 6 .. 415-417(v.17), df. 417

recreation, purpose of, ch. 6 .. 417(v.17)

reduction of activity, ch. 4 .. 295(v.27)

refined activity, ch. 3 .. 211(v.19); ch. 4 .. 313(v.38), 315(v.38); ch. 5 .. 332(v.2), 348(v.11)

refined qualities of feeling, ch. 4 .. 315(v.38)

refinement of breath, ch. 4 .. 295(v.27), 298-299(v.29-30); ch. 6 .. 407(v.12)

refinement of the nervous system, ch. 6 .. 439-440(v.28), 466(v.46)

reflection of Being, ch. 2 .. 166(v.66)

regaining of individual existence, ch. 6 .. 464(v.45)

reincarnation (see also cycle of birth and death), ch. 2 .. 92(v.13); ch. 4 .. 259-260(v.5), 265(v.9); ch. 6 .. 461-462(v.41-43), 464-465(v.45)

relationship of Absolute and God, ch. 6 .. 444(v.30)

relationship of Absolute and relative, ch. 2 .. 95(v.15); ch. 3 .. 178-179(v.1), 183(v.3), 215(v.22); ch. 4 .. 307(v.35); ch. 5 .. 339(v.7), 344(v.10), 351(v.14), 356(v.16), 367 (v.22); ch. 6 .. 442(v.29), 449(v.32)

relationship of action and renunciation, ch. 5 .. 327-329(intro.)

relationship of action to cosmic consciousness, ch. 4 .. 290-292 (v.24)

relationship of faith and knowledge, ch. 4 .. 318-319(v.40)

relationship of knowledge and *dharma,* ch. 3 .. 181(v.1)

relationship of man and God, ch. 6 .. 443-450(v.30-32)

relationship of master and pupil (see also teaching), ch. 2 .. 85-86(v.7), 89-91(v.10-11), 104(v.26); ch. 3 .. 178-179(v.1), 182(v.2); ch. 4 .. 258-259(v.3-4), 261(v.6), 303-305(v.34); ch. 5 .. 330(v.1); ch. 6 .. 459(v.39)

relationship of mind and nervous system, ch. 6 .. 390(v.3)

relationship of *Sankhya* and *Yoga,* ch. 5 .. 335-336(v.4-5), 355-356 (v.16-17), 366(v.21)

relationship of self and Self, ch. 6 .. 395-399(v.5-7)

relationship of *Yoga* and renunciation, ch. 5 .. 331(v.1); ch. 6 .. 385-389(v.1-2)

relationship with others, ch. 2 .. 115(v.38)

relative, ch. 2 .. 98-99(v.19-20), 104-105(v.27), 126-132(v.45), 133(v.47), 142(v.50), 172-173(v.71-72); ch. 3 .. 177-179 (intro.-v.1), 188-189(v.5-6), 192-195(v.8-9), 198(v.11), 200 (v.12), 204(v.14), 211(v.19), 213(v.20), 215-216(v.22), 219(v.26), 225(v.30), 228(v.32), 233(v.35), 239(v.39), 244 (v.43); ch. 4 .. 249(intro.), 251(v.1), 253(v.1), 262-263 (v.7), 275(v.16), 279(v.18), 286-287(v.20-21), 291(v.24), 302(v.33), 304(v.34), 307(v.35), 309(v.36), 312-313(v.38); ch. 5 .. 332-333(v.2-3), 337-342(v.6-9), 354(v.15), 356 (v.16), 358-359(v.17-18), 362(v.20), 365(v.21), 367-368 (v.22-23), 370(v.23), 372-373(v.24), 375(v.26); ch. 6 .. 391(v.3), 394(v.4), 397-398(v.6), 407(v.12), 423(v.20), 425-426(v.21-22), 430(v.24), 432(v.25), 435(v.26), 440 (v.28), 452(v.35), 454(v.36), 460(v.41), 463(v.44), 467 (v.47)

relative and Absolute, junction-point of, ch. 6 .. 437-438(v.27)

relativity and God, ch. 3 .. 215(v.22)

religion, ch. 4 .. 256(v.2); ch. 6 .. 449(v.32)

religious performance, ch. 3 .. 194(v.9)

renunciation, ch. 2 .. 143-145(v.57), 153(v.55), 174(v.72); ch. 3 .. 186-187(v.3-4), 244(v.43); ch. 4 .. 250(intro.), 319-320

(v.41), 322(v.42); ch. 5 .. 325-334(intro.-v.3), 336-338
(v.5-6), 350-353(v.13-14), 357-358(v.17), 363(v.20), 365
(v.21), 370-373(v.23-25), 375(v.26), 378-380(v.28-29);
ch. 6 .. 385(v.1), 389(v.2), 396(v.5), 400(v.8)

renunciation and action, relationship of, ch. 5 .. 327-329(intro.)

renunciation and *Yoga,* relationship of, ch. 5 .. 331(v.1); ch. 6 ..
385-389(v.1-2)

renunciation, four interpretations of, ch. 5 .. 331-332(v.2)

renunciation, glory of, ch. 5 .. 353(v.14), 379-380(v.29)

renunciation, knowledge of, ch. 5 .. 325-326(intro.), 353(v.14)

renunciation, man of (see also *sanyasi*), ch. 5 .. 333-334(v.3)

renunciation, perfect, ch. 5 .. 327(intro.), 332(v.2), 351(v.14),
378(v.28)

renunciation, philosophy of, ch. 5 .. 327-328(intro.), 373(v.25),
378(v.28)

renunciation, practising, ch. 5 .. 326(intro.)

renunciation, *Yoga* of, ch. 5 .. 327-328(intro.), 365(v.21)

resistance of desire, ch. 1 .. 56(v.32)

resistance to development of cosmic consciousness, ch. 3 .. 191
(v.8)

resolute intellect (see also established intellect, steady intellect),
ch. 2 .. 121-122(v.41), 124-126(v.44-45), 147(v.53), 168
(v.68); ch. 3 .. 179(v.1); ch. 6 .. 399(v.7), 423(v.20)

response of nature, ch. 3 .. 199(v.12)

responsibility, individual, ch. 6 .. 395-397(v.5)

restful alertness, ch. 2 .. 168(v.68), 173(v.72); ch. 4 .. 313(v.38);
ch. 5 .. 346(v.11), 369(v.23); ch. 6 .. 393(v.3), 407(v.12),
417(v.17), 429(v.24)

restraining the organs of action, ch. 3 .. 189(v.6)

restraint (see also control), ch. 3 .. 189(v.6), 229-231(v.33-34),
241-242(v.41); ch. 4 .. 294(v.26); ch. 6 .. 455(v.36)

restraint, idea of, ch. 3 .. 231(v.34)

result of action, ch. 2 .. 115(v.38), 134(v.47), 139-140(v.49);
ch. 3 .. 218(v.25)

retarding evolution, ch. 3 .. 233(v.35)

revelation, ch. 2 .. 120(v.40)

revelation, divine, ch. 4 .. 264(v.8)

revival, ch. 4 .. 255-258(v.2-3)

right action (see also good action), ch. 2 .. 84(v.7); ch. 3 .. 191-
193(v.8), 200-203(v.13), 219-220(v.26); ch. 4 .. 276(v.17),
294(v.26), 296(v.27); ch. 6 .. 390(v.3), 427(v.23), 466(v.46)

right action, basis of, ch. 4 .. 294(v.26)

right action, spontaneous, ch. 3 .. 192(v.8)

right and wrong, ch. 1 .. 61-62(v.37), 63(v.39); ch. 2 .. 114(v.38), 127-130(v.45), 142(v.50), 146-147(v.52-53); ch. 3 .. 219-220(v.26)

righteous behaviour (see also good action, right action), ch. 1 .. 36(v.14), 63(v.39); ch. 6 .. 460(v.41)

righteous, desire of the, ch. 4 .. 264(v.8)

righteous, worlds of the, ch. 6 .. 460-461(v.41)

righteousness (see also virtue), ch. 1 .. 38-39(v.15), 42-43(v.21), 52-54(v.29-30), 63-64(v.39-40), 70(v.45); ch. 2 .. 127(v.45); ch. 3 .. 200-203(v.13); ch. 4 .. 252(v.1), 257(v.2), 263-265(v.7-9); ch. 6 .. 390(v.3), 460-461(v.41)

rites and ceremonies, ch. 1 .. 67(v.42); ch. 2 .. 123-124(v.42-43), 132(v.46); ch. 3 .. 194-195(v.9), 198(v.11), 203-206(v.13-15); ch. 4 .. 268(v.12), 290(v.24), 297(v.28); ch. 6 .. 463 (v.44), 466(v.46)

routine of daily life, ch. 6 .. 415-416(v.16-17), 453(v.35)

Royal *Yoga* of Lord *Krishna,* ch. 6 .. 383(intro.)

sage, ch. 2 .. 154-155(v.56), 169-170(v.69); ch. 4 .. 252(v.1), 255(v.2); ch. 5 .. 336-338(v.6), 377-378(v.28); ch. 6 .. 444(v.30)

saints and God, communion of, ch. 6 .. 444(v.30)

sakshi-kutastha (silent witness), ch. 5 .. 350(v.13)

samadhi (transcendental consciousness), ch. 2 .. 144(v.51), 147-148(v.53), 150(v.55), 153(v.55); ch. 4 .. 313(v.38), 321 (v.42); ch. 5 .. 345-346(v.11); ch. 6 .. 402(v.10)

samadhi, nirvikalpa (cosmic consciousness), ch. 4 .. 317(v.39)

samadhi, savikalpa (transcendental consciousness), ch. 4 .. 317 (v.39)

sankalpa (incentive of desire), ch. 6 .. 388-391(v.2-3)

Sankhya (wisdom of absolute and relative), ch. 1 .. 66(v.41); ch. 2 .. 91-95(v.11-15), 111(v.34), 113-117(v.37-39), 128 (v.45), 149-150(v.54); ch. 3 .. 185(v.3), 223(v.28), 239 (v.39); ch. 4 .. 249(intro.), 251(v.1), 272(v.14), 275(v.16), 290(v.23), 322(v.42); ch. 5 .. 326-328(intro.), 330(v.1), 334-336(v.3-5), 355-356(v.16-17), 361(v.19), 363(v.20), 373-374(v.25-26), 376(v.26); ch. 6 .. 384(intro.), 401(v.9), 420(v.18)

Sankhya and *Yoga,* relationship of, ch. 5 .. 335-336(v.4-5), 355-356(v.16-17), 366(v.21)

Sankhya, essence of, ch. 2 .. 91-95(v.12-15), 117(v.39)

Sankhya, technique of teaching, ch. 4 .. 275(v.16)

Sanyasa (renunciation of action), ch. 5 .. 331-332(v.2), 334(v.3), 337-338(v.6), 349(v.12); ch. 6 .. 385-389(v.1-2)

sanyasi (recluse), ch. 3 .. 185(v.3); ch. 4 .. 257(v.2); ch. 5 .. 333-334(v.3); ch. 6 .. 384-389(v.1-2)

sanyasi, criteria of a, ch. 5 .. 333-334(v.3); ch. 6 .. 384-389(v.1-2)

Sat-Chit-Ananda (absolute bliss-consciousness), ch. 3 .. 187(v.4); ch. 6 .. 441(v.28)

Sat-Yuga, ch. 4 .. 254(v.1)

sattva (purity; creative *guna*), ch. 1 .. 37(v.14); ch. 2 .. 128 (v.45); ch. 3 .. 220(v.27), 224(v.29), 237(v.37); ch. 4 .. 262(v.7), 269(v.13), 306(v.35); ch. 5 .. 359-360(v.18)

savikalpa samadhi (transcendental consciousness), ch. 4 .. 317 (v.39)

schools of thought, ch. 2 .. 147(v.53); ch. 6 .. 450(v.32)

science and art of successful living, ch. 4 .. 255(v.2)

science of action, ch. 3 .. 245(v.43); ch. 4 .. 280-290(v.18-23)

scriptures, ch. 1 .. 50(v.28); ch. 2 .. 146(v.52), 148(v.53); ch. 3 .. 192(v.8); ch. 4 .. 297(v.28), 305(v.34); ch. 6 .. 427 (v.23), 447(v.31)

search for happiness, ch. 2 .. 118-119(v.40), 121(v.41), 133(v.46), 166(v.66); ch. 3 .. 239(v.39); ch. 4 .. 267(v.11); ch. 5 .. 333(v.3), 371(v.24)

seat of desire, ch. 3 .. 240-242(v.40-41)

seclusion, ch. 6 .. 402-403(v.10)

second element, principle of the, ch. 2 .. 126(v.45)

second manifestation of creation, ch. 3 .. 206(v.15)

secret, supreme, ch. 4 .. 258(v.3)

seed of action, ch. 2 .. 143(v.50); ch. 4 .. 286(v.20), 311(v.37)

seed of desire, ch. 2 .. 142(v.50), 158(v.58); ch. 5 .. 341(v.7); ch. 6 .. 388-389(v.2), 394(v.4), 422(v.19)

seekers of God, ch. 4 .. 272-273(v.15)

seekers of liberation, ch. 4 .. 272-273(v.15)

seers, ch. 5 .. 373-374(v.25)

self, ch. 3 .. 187(v.4), 202(v.13), 212(v.19), 228(v.32), 236-237 (v.37), 239(v.39), 243(v.43); ch. 4 .. 259(v.5), 266(v.10); ch. 5 .. 338-339(v.7), df. 339(v.7), 349(v.12), 358(v.17),

364(v.21), 368(v.22), 370(v.23); ch. 6 .. 395-399(v.5-7),
    407(v.12), 441-443(v.29)

Self (see also Being), ch. 1 .. 37(v.14); ch. 2 .. 92(v.12), 98(v.18-
    19), 120(v.40), 126-132(v.45), 143-145(v.51), 147-154
    (v.53-55), 165(v.66); ch. 3 .. 179-180(v.1), 187(v.4), 193-
    194(v.8-9), 202(v.13), 204(v.14), 208(v.17), 212-214(v.19-
    20), 219(v.26), 221-231(v.27-34), 233-237(v.35-37), 241-
    243(v.40-43); ch. 4 .. 259(v.5), 266(v.10), 287-288(v.21-22),
    296(v.27), 306-307(v.35), 309(v.36), 319-321(v.41); ch. 5 ..
    326(intro.), 337-342(v.6-9), df. 339(v.7), 346-347(v.11),
    349-350(v.12-13), 352-355(v.14-16), 359-360(v.18), 362
    (v.20), 364-366(v.21-22), 368-369(v.22-23), 372-376(v.24-
    26); ch. 6 .. 392-399(v.3-7), 404(v.10), 406-407(v.12), 409
    (v.14), 411(v.14), 418-419(v.18), 421-427(v.19-23), 430
    (v.24), 432-435(v.25-26), 441-442(v.29), 444(v.30), 447-
    449(v.32), 454(v.36), 467-468(v.47)

Self, all beings in the, ch. 4 .. 305-308(v.35); ch. 5 .. 338-341
    (v.7); ch. 6 .. 441-442(v.29)

Self and activity, separation of (see also cosmic consciousness),
    ch. 2 .. 150-151(v.55), 155-157(v.56-57), 160(v.59), 162
    (v.61), 170(v.70), 172(v.71); ch. 3 .. 179-180(v.1), 187
    (v.4), 193-194(v.8-9), 198-200(v.11-12), 202(v.13), 204
    (v.14), 208(v.17), 210-212(v.19), 218-219(v.25-26), 221
    (v.27), 223(v.28), 225-228(v.30-32), 230-231(v.33-34), 235
    (v.36), 237(v.37), 239-240(v.39); ch. 4 .. 249-250(intro.),
    266(v.10), 272-274(v.14-16), 280-286(v.18-20), 302(v.33),
    305-307(v.35), 310(v.37), 312-314(v.38), 320(v.41), 322
    (v.42); ch. 5 .. 325-327(intro.), 332-334(v.2-3), 336-339
    (v.5-7), 341-343(v.7-9), 345-347(v.10-11), 349-353(v.12-
    14), 355-356(v.16), 360-361(v.18-19), 363-365(v.20-21),
    367-368(v.22-23), 370(v.23), 372-373(v.24-25), 375-376
    (v.26), 378(v.28); ch. 6 .. 385(v.1), 391-392(v.3), 398(v.6),
    407(v.12), 419(v.18), 426(v.22), 434(v.25), 453(v.35),
    455(v.36)

Self and activity, unity of, ch. 3 .. 193(v.8), 211(v.19); ch. 4 ..
    307(v.35); ch. 5 .. 332(v.2), 347(v.11)

self and Self, relationship of, ch. 6 .. 395-399(v.5-7)

self and Self, union of, ch. 5 .. 339-340(v.7)

Self-awareness, ch. 2 .. 144(v.51), 171(v.70); ch. 3 .. 208(v.17);
    ch. 4 .. 249(intro.), 314(v.38); ch. 6 .. 392-393(v.3)

Self-consciousness (see also transcendental consciousness), ch. 2 ..
    144-145(v.51), 147(v.53), 151(v.55), 173(v.72); ch. 3 ..
    187(v.4), 191(v.8), 209-212(v.18-19), 226(v.30), 236(v.37);
    ch. 4 .. 293(v.25), 306(v.35), 313(v.38), 317(v.39); ch. 5 ..

326(intro.), 332(v.2), 344(v.10), 348-349(v.12), 372(v.24), 375(v.26); ch. 6 .. 385(v.1), 395-396(v.5), 402(v.10), 422 (v.19), 428(v.23), 434(v.25), 467(v.47)

self-contained feeling, ch. 3 .. 220(v.27)

self-control, ch. 4 .. 295-296(v.27); ch. 5 .. 373(v.25)

self-deception, ch. 2 .. 139(v.49)

Self, *dharma* of the, ch. 3 .. 233-235(v.35-36)

self-disciplined, ch. 2 .. 164(v.64)

Self, identified with, ch. 2 .. 151(v.55)

self-illuminant effulgence of life, ch. 3 .. 206(v.15)

Self in all beings, ch. 6 .. 441-442(v.29)

Self in Union with God, ch. 3 .. 211-212(v.19)

Self, loss of the, ch. 3 .. 213(v.20)

self, mastery of the, ch. 5 .. 340(v.7)

Self, mastery of the, ch. 5 .. 339-341(v.7)

Self, possessed of the, ch. 4 .. 319-321(v.41)

self-purification, ch. 6 .. 406-407(v.12)

Self seen in God, ch. 4 .. 307(v.35)

self-sufficient, ch. 2 .. 137(v.48); ch. 4 .. 284(v.19); ch. 5 .. 340 (v.7), 363(v.20), 372(v.24); ch. 6 .. 394(v.4), 424(v.20)

Self, thinking of the, ch. 3 .. 185(v.3)

selfishness, ch. 1 .. 56(v.32); ch. 3 .. 201(v.13), 209(v.18); ch. 5 .. 374(v.25)

sense, engaging one, ch. 2 .. 162(v.61)

sense of progress, ch. 2 .. 125(v.44)

sense of proportion, ch. 2 .. 130(v.45)

sense of sight, ch. 6 .. 408(v.13)

sense of values (see also values), ch. 3 .. 199(v.12); ch. 6 .. 453-454(v.35-36)

senseless, ch. 3 .. 228(v.32)

senses, ch. 1 .. 37(v.14), 53(v.29), 57(v.32); ch. 2 .. 87-89(v.8-10), 93(v.14), 98(v.18), 107(v.29), 124(v.43), 140(v.49), 158-164(v.58-64), 167-170(v.67-69); ch. 3 .. 186(v.3), 189-190(v.6-7), 201(v.13), 204(v.14), 207(v.16), 211(v.19), 223(v.28), 230-231(v.33-34), 237(v.37), 240-244(v.39-43); ch. 4 .. 264(v.8), 266(v.10), 278(v.18), 284(v.19), 286-287 (v.20-21), 291(v.24), 293-296(v.26-27), 311(v.37), 313 (v.38), 315-318(v.38-39); ch. 5 .. 335(v.4), 338-344(v.7-9), 345-348(v.11), 362(v.20), 364-368(v.21-22), 372(v.24), 376-378(v.27-28); ch. 6 .. 393-394(v.4), 398(v.6), 400

(v.8), 406-410(v.12-14), 412-416(v.15-17), 420-422(v.18-19), 424-425(v.21), 429-431(v.24), 443-445(v.30-31), 451 (v.34), 455(v.36), 467-468(v.47)

senses and organs of action in *Karma Yoga,* ch. 3 .. 190(v.7)

senses, beyond the, ch. 6 .. 424-425(v.21)

senses, calming the, ch. 4 .. 294(v.26)

senses, conquered, ch. 5 .. 338-341(v.7)

senses, contact of the, ch. 2 .. 93-95(v.14-15); ch. 3 .. 236(v.37); ch. 4 .. 284(v.19); ch. 5 .. 365-366(v.21-22), 376-377 (v.27); ch. 6 .. 419(v.18)

senses, control of the, ch. 2 .. 160-162(v.59-61), 164(v.64); ch. 3 .. 189-190(v.6-7), 244(v.43); ch. 4 .. 294-295(v.26-27); ch. 5 .. 377(v.27); ch. 6 .. 429-431(v.24)

senses, desired direction of, ch. 4 .. 295-296(v.27)

senses, feeding of the, ch. 2 .. 159-161(v.59); ch. 4 .. 294(v.26), 298(v.30); ch. 6 .. 414-415(v.16)

senses, finer levels of the, ch. 2 .. 160(v.59), 162(v.61), 168-169 (v.68)

senses, full development of the, ch. 6 .. 416(v.17)

senses, God on level of, ch. 4 .. 264(v.8); ch. 6 .. 444(v.30), 468 (v.47)

senses, highest capacity of the, ch. 5 .. 343(v.8,9)

senses, influence of the, ch. 6 .. 421(v.19), 451(v.34)

senses, joys of the, ch. 5 .. 365-368(v.21-22)

senses, mastery of the, ch. 2 .. 160(v.59); ch. 5 .. 340-341(v.7); ch. 6 .. 400(v.8)

senses, natural tendency of the, ch. 6 .. 431(v.24)

senses, non-indulgence of the, ch. 2 .. 159(v.58)

senses, objects of the, ch. 2 .. 158-161(v.58-60), 163-164)v.62-64), 167-169(v.67-68); ch. 3 .. 189-190(v.6-7), 230-231(v.34), 236(v.37); ch. 4 .. 264(v.8), 266(v.10), 293-294(v.26), 298 (v.30); ch. 5 .. 342-343(v.8,9), 362(v.20), 364-368(v.21-22), 377(v.27); ch. 6 .. 393-394(v.4), 396(v.5), 407(v.12), 414-415(v.16), 420-422(v.18-19), 455(v.36)

senses of perception, ch. 3 .. 190(v.7); ch. 5 .. 341(v.7); ch. 6 .. 429(v.24)

senses, organized, ch. 3 .. 190(v.7), 241-243(v.41-42)

senses, origin of the, ch. 6 .. 424-425(v.21)

senses, proper use of the, ch. 4 .. 294(v.26)

senses, stilling the, ch. 6 .. 408(v.13)

senses, subdued, ch. 2 .. 161-163(v.61); ch. 4 .. 316-318(v.39); ch. 6 .. 406-407(v.12)

senses, taste for, ch. 2 .. 159-161(v.59)

senses, turbulent, ch. 2 .. 161(v.60)

senses: turn inwards, ch. 4 .. 294(v.26)

senses, village of the, ch. 6 .. 429-431(v.24)

senses, withdrawal of the, ch. 2 .. 158-159(v.58), 168-169(v.68)

sensory experience, ch. 2 .. 121(v.41); ch. 3 .. 237(v.37); ch. 5 ..
    362(v.20); ch. 6 .. 425(v.21)

sensory level, action on the, ch. 3 .. 183-184(v.3)

sensory level, Being on the, ch. 2 .. 159-161(v.58-59); ch. 6 .. 443
    (v.30), 467-468(v.47)

separation of Self from activity (see also cosmic consciousness),
    ch. 2 .. 150-151(v.55), 155-157(v.56-57), 160(v.59), 162
    (v.61), 170(v.70), 172(v.71); ch. 3 .. 179-180(v.1), 187
    (v.4), 193-194(v.8-9), 198-200(v.11-12), 202(v.13), 204
    (v.14), 208(v.17), 210-212(v.19), 218-219(v.25-26), 221
    (v.27), 223(v.28), 225-228(v.30-32), 230-231(v.33-34), 235
    (v.36), 237(v.37), 239-240(v.39); ch. 4 .. 249-250(intro.),
    266(v.10), 272-274(v.14-16), 280-286(v.18-20), 302(v.33),
    305-307(v.35), 310(v.37), 312-314(v.38), 320(v.41), 322
    (v.42); ch. 5 .. 325-327(intro.), 332-334(v.2-3), 336-339
    (v.5-7), 341-343(v.7-9), 345-347(v.10-11), 349-353(v.12-
    14), 355-356(v.20-21), 367-368(v.22-23), 370(v.23), 372-
    373(v.24-25), 375-376(v.26), 378(v.28); ch. 6 .. 385(v.1),
    391-392(v.3), 398(v.6), 407(v.12), 419(v.18), 426(v.22),
    434(v.25), 453(v.35), 455(v.36)

service, ch. 4 .. 303-305(v.34), df. 304(v.34), 315(v.38)

Shakhas (branches of the *Vedas*), ch. 3 .. 195(v.9)

Shankara, ch. 2 .. 152-153(v.55); ch. 4 .. 256-257(v.2), 305
    (v.34); ch. 6 .. 408(v.13)

Shankaracharya tradition, ch. 4 .. 256-257(v.2)

Shiva, ch. 4 .. 253(v.1)

shock, ch. 2 .. 79(v.2)

short cut, ch. 6 .. 456(v.37)

shreyas (evolution or fulfilment), ch. 1 .. 55(v.31)

sight, sense of, ch. 6 .. 408(v.13)

silence, ch. 4 .. 278-279(v.18), 282-283(v.19), 286(v.20), 298
    (v.29), 313-314(v.38); ch. 5 .. 340(v.7), 369(v.23); ch. 6 ..
    391-393(v.3), 397(v.5), 401(v.9), 409(v.14), 419(v.18)

silence and activity, ch. 4 .. 278-279(v.18), 282(v.19), 286(v.20),
    313-314(v.38); ch. 5 .. 340(v.7); ch. 6 .. 392(v.3), 428
    (v.23)

silence of Godhead, ch. 6 .. 392(v.3)

silence of Unity, ch. 6 .. 391-392(v.3)

silence, quality of, ch. 6 .. 392(v.3)

silence, three states of, ch. 6 .. 392(v.3)

silent witness, ch. 2 .. 98(v.19); ch. 4 .. 291(v.24); ch. 5 .. 350 (v.13), 354(v.15)

simplicity of transcendental meditation (see also automatic, easy), ch. 2 .. 117-120(v.40), 144(v.51); ch. 5 .. 377(v.27)

sin (see also wrong action), ch. 1 .. 60-61(v.36), 70-71(v.45-46); ch. 2 .. 109-110(v.33), df. 110(v.33), 113-115(v.38); ch. 3 .. 180(v.1), 200-203(v.13), df. 202(v.13), 207(v.15-16), 216(v.23), 227(v.31), 235(v.36); ch. 4 .. 286-287(v.21), 298-299(v.30), 308-309(v.36); ch. 5 .. 344-345(v.10), 354 (v.15), 356(v.16), 373(v.25); ch. 6 .. 460(v.41), 464(v.45)

sin against God, ch. 3 .. 207(v.16); ch. 6 .. 449-450(v.32)

sin, purified of all, ch. 6 .. 464(v.45)

sinless (see also purity), ch. 6 .. 437(v.27)

six systems, ch. 2 .. 116(v.39)

skill in action, ch. 2 .. 141-143(v.50), 147-148(v.53); ch. 3 .. 190 (v.7)

skill in teaching (see also teaching), ch. 3 .. 216(v.22)

skill of the discourse, ch. 3 .. 215(v.21), 226(v.30); ch. 4 .. 278 (v.17), 302(v.33); ch. 5 .. 327-328(intro.); ch. 6 .. 426 (v.22), 442(v.29)

sleep, ch. 1 .. 45(v.24); ch. 3 .. 184(v.3), 187-188(v.4-5), 208 (v.17); ch. 4 .. 277(v.17), 314(v.38), 317(v.39), ch. 5 .. 338-340(v.7); ch. 6 .. 406(v.12), 409(v.14), 413-416(v.15-17)

social behaviour, ch. 2 .. 110(v.33)

social disorder, ch. 1 .. 66-67(v.42), 70(v.45); ch. 4 .. 262-263 (v.7)

social influence, ch. 2 .. 110-111(v.33-34)

social order, ch. 1 .. 66-67(v.42), 70(v.45); ch. 2 .. 110(v.33); ch. 3 .. 191(v.8)

society, division of (see also caste), ch. 3 .. 191-192(v.8)

solution to any problem, ch. 3 .. 234(v.35)

sorrow (see also suffering), ch. 1 .. 71-72(v.47); ch. 2 .. 76-78 (v.1), 154-155(v.56), 165(v.65); ch. 4 .. 309(v.36); ch. 5 .. 366-368(v.22); ch. 6 .. 415-418(v.17), 424(v.20), 425-428 (v.22-23)

sorrow in heart, ch. 2 .. 155(v.56)

sorrow in mind, ch. 2 .. 155(v.56)

sorrow, sources of (see also source of suffering), ch. 5 .. 366-368 (v.22), 370(v.23)

source of all activity, ch. 3 . . 206(v.15)

source of all suffering, ch. 4 . . 318(v.40)

source of all weakness, ch. 4 . . 318(v.40)

source of creation, ch. 3 . . 206(v.15), 207(v.16); ch. 4 . . 270-271(v.13-14)

source of desire, ch. 3 . . 238(v.38)

sources of sorrow, ch. 5 . . 366-368(v.22), 370(v.23)

space, ch. 2 . . 99(v.20); ch. 4 . . 260(v.5), 276(v.17)

speaking ill of others, ch. 3 . . 227(v.31)

speech, ch. 3 . . 214(v.20); ch. 5 . . 369(v.23); ch. 6 . . 421(v.19), 440-441(v.28)

spirit, ch. 2 . . 96-101(v.17-23); ch. 5 . . 343(v.8,9); ch. 6 . . 407 (v.12)

spirit, pure of, ch. 5 . . 338(v.7)

spiritual decadence, ch. 4 . . 257(v.2)

spiritual development, ch. 3 . . 185(v.3); ch. 4 . . 255(v.2), 318 (v.40)

spiritual life, ch. 2 . . 87(v.8), 153(v.55), 156(v.57); ch. 3 . . 214 (v.20); ch. 5 . . 359(v.18); ch. 6 . . 395(v.5)

spontaneous right action, ch. 3 . . 192(v.8)

spur to activity, ch. 2 . . 128(v.45); ch. 3 . . 236(v.37); ch. 5 . . 349(v.12); ch. 6 . . 437-438(v.27)

stability, ch. 3 . . 237(v.37); ch. 4 . . 317(v.39); ch. 5 . . 343(v.8,9), 351(v.14), 361(v.19); ch. 6 . . 387(v.1)

stages of action, ch. 2 . . 118(v.40)

stages of evolution (see also level of consciousness, level of evolution), ch. 3 . . 193(v.8), 231-232(v.35), 234(v.35)

stages of the mind, ch. 2 . . 166(v.66)

start of a thought, ch. 4 . . 282(v.19)

start of action, ch. 3 . . 213(v.20); ch. 4 . . 281-283(v.19)

state of Divinity, ch. 4 . . 265(v.9), 267(v.11)

steadiness of mind (see also steady intellect), ch. 2 . . 166-167 (v.66); ch. 6 . . 390(v.3), 452-453(v.35)

steady, art of being, ch. 6 . . 408(v.13)

steady intellect (see also balanced intellect, established intellect), ch. 2 . . 148-161(v.54-59); ch. 5 . . 361-363(v.20); ch. 6 . . 422-424(v.19-20)

steady intellect, essentials of, ch. 2 . . 150-161(v.55-59)

stilling the body, ch. 6 . . 408(v.13)

stilling the senses, ch. 6 . . 408(v.13)

stimulus, outer, ch. 3 .. 238(v.38)

stopping transcendental meditation, ch. 6 .. 457-461(v.38-41)

storehouse of impressions (see also *sankalpa*), ch. 4 .. 281-287 (v.19-21), 311(v.37); ch. 6 .. 422(v.19)

strain, ch. 3 .. 186(v.3), 189(v.6), 191-192(v.8), 229(v.33); ch. 5 .. 377(v.27); ch. 6 .. 403-404(v.10), 413(v.15), 418(v.17), 431(v.24), 436(v.26), 446(v.31), 454(v.36), 466(v.46)

strength, ch. 1 .. 46(v.25); ch. 4 .. 263(v.8); ch. 5 .. 350(v.13); ch. 6 .. 463(v.44)

stress and strain (see also tension), ch. 2 .. 156(v.57); ch. 3 .. 229 (v.33); ch. 6 .. 403(v.10)

struggle, ch. 1 .. 66(v.41)

student, ch. 2 .. 85-86(v.7)

subdued mind and body, ch. 6 .. 402-405(v.10)

subdued senses, ch. 2 .. 161-163(v.61); ch. 4 .. 316-318(v.39); ch. 6 .. 406-407(v.12)

subdued thought, ch. 6 .. 421-422(v.19)

subduing desires, ch. 3 .. 243-245(v.43)

subject and object, ch. 3 .. 191(v.8); ch. 5 .. 343-344(v.8,9)

subjective, ch. 2 .. 154-155(v.56), 164(v.63); ch. 3 .. 222(v.28), 240(v.40), 243(v.42); ch. 5 .. 352(v.14)

submission (see also surrender), ch. 4 .. 303-305(v.34)

submission to Being, ch. 4 .. 304(v.34)

subtle, ch. 2 .. 129(v.45), 160(v.59), 162(v.61), 166(v.66), 168-169(v.68); ch. 3 .. 192(v.8), 195(v.9), 198(v.11), 203(v.13), 205-207(v.14-16), 210(v.19), 213-214(v.20), 219(v.26), 242-243(v.42); ch. 4 .. 266(v.10), 275(v.16), 282(v.19), 293(v.25), 295(v.27); ch. 5 .. 338-339(v.7), 347(v.11); ch. 6 .. 390(v.3), 403-407(v.10-12), 412-413(v.15), 425 (v.21), 430(v.24), 432-433(v.25), 437(v.27)

subtle and gross, ch. 2 .. 129(v.45), 160(v.59), 168-169(v.68); ch. 3 .. 195(v.9), 197(v.11), 200(v.12), 207(v.16), 213 (v.20), 219(v.26); ch. 4 .. 279(v.18); ch. 5 .. 332(v.2), 339 (v.7), 360(v.19); ch. 6 .. 390(v.3), 394(v.4), 403(v.10), 421(v.19), 433(v.25)

subtle aspect of *yagya*, ch. 3 .. 195(v.9), 205(v.14)

subtlest level of creation, ch. 2 .. 169(v.68); ch. 3 .. 222(v.28)

success (see also prosperity), ch. 3 .. 214(v.20); ch. 4 .. 268 (v.12); ch. 5 .. 361(v.19)

success in action, ch. 4 .. 250(intro.)

success in the practice of *Yoga*, ch. 6 .. 415(v.16), 454(v.36)

successful living, science and art of, ch. 4 .. 255(v.2)

sufferer, ch. 2 .. 98(v.18)

suffering (see also sorrow), ch. 1 .. 27(v.1), 49-52(v.28), 54 (v.30), 61(v.36), 66(v.41); ch. 2 .. 87(v.8), 110(v.33), 165 (v.65); ch. 3 .. 198(v.11), 202(v.13), 228(v.32), 237(v.37); ch. 4 .. 250(intro.), 274(v.16), 309(v.36), 312(v.38), 318 (v.40); ch. 5 .. 353(v.14), 356(v.16), 366-368(v.22); ch. 6 .. 418(v.17), 426-427(v.22-23)

suffering, source of, ch. 4 .. 318(v.40)

superiority of a *yogi,* ch. 6 .. 465-466(v.46)

superiority of *Karma Yoga,* ch. 5 .. 332-333(v.2)

superstitions, ch. 3 .. 199(v.12)

support of nature, ch. 2 .. 133(v.46); ch. 3 .. 197(v.1), 233-234 (v.35); ch. 5 .. 350(v.13), 375(v.26); ch. 6 .. 463(v.44)

supporter of all, ch. 6 .. 449(v.32)

Supreme (see also Divine), ch. 2 .. 159-162(v.59-61); ch. 3 .. 210-212(v.19), 225(v.30), 244(v.43); ch. 4 .. 294(v.26); ch. 5 .. 379(v.29); ch. 6 .. 399(v.7), 428(v.23), 466(v.46), 468(v.47)

supreme good, ch. 5 .. 331-333(v.2)

supreme happiness, ch. 3 .. 229(v.33); ch. 5 .. 380(v.29); ch. 6 .. 428(v.23), 436-438(v.26-27)

supreme knowledge, ch. 4 .. 255(v.1), 315-316(v.38); ch. 5 .. 354(v.15)

supreme level of creation, ch. 6 .. 446(v.31)

supreme liberation, ch. 6 .. 412-414(v.15)

Supreme, non-involvement of the, ch. 4 .. 272(v.14), 275(v.16); ch. 5 .. 354(v.15)

supreme secret, ch. 4 .. 258(v.3)

surrender (see also devotion), ch. 2 .. 83-88(v.6-9), 104(v.26), 131(v.45); ch. 3 .. 198(v.11), 225-227(v.30); ch. 4 .. 267 (v.11), 272(v.14), 303-305(v.34); ch. 5 .. 330(v.1), 344 (v.10), 352-353(v.14), 380(v.29); ch. 6 .. 411-412(v.14), 424-425(v.20-21), 446(v.31)

surrender of action to God, ch. 3 .. 226(v.30); ch. 5 .. 352-353 (v.14); ch. 6 .. 411(v.14)

suspension, ch. 1 .. 51(v.28), 53(v.29); ch. 2 .. 76-79(v.1-2), 87 (v.8), 112(v.35), 129(v.45), 146(v.52); ch. 3 .. 182(v.2)

suspension of breathing, ch. 4 .. 298(v.29); ch. 5 .. 377(v.27)

sword of knowledge, ch. 4 .. 321-322(v.42)

Taittiriya Upanishad, ch. 6 .. 461(v.41)

tamas (destructive *guna*), ch. 2 .. 128(v.45); ch. 3 .. 220(v.27), 224(v.29), 237(v.37); ch. 4 .. 262(v.7), 269(v.13), 306 (v.35); ch. 5 .. 359-360(v.18); ch. 6 .. 424(v.21)

'*tanmatras*', ch. 6 .. 424-425(v.21)

'*Tat tvam asi*' ('That thou art'), ch. 5 .. 357(v.17)

teaching, ch. 1 .. 46-47(v.25), 67(v.42); ch. 2 .. 85-86(v.7), 89-92(v.10-12), 100(v.21), 102-104(v.24-26), 106(v.29), 111-113(v.34-37), 116-123(v.39-42), 127(v.45), 130-131(v.45), 150(v.55); ch. 3 .. 178-183(v.1-2), 216(v.22), 218-220 (v.26), 224(v.29), 227(v.31), 229(v.33); ch. 4 .. 260-261 (v.6), 273(v.15), 275(v.16), 302(v.33), 317(v.39); ch. 5 .. 352(v.14); ch. 6 .. 421(v.19), 436(v.26)

teaching, purity of, ch. 4 .. 255-257(v.2)

teaching, skill in (see also skill of the discourse), ch. 3 .. 216(v.22)

teaching the ignorant, ch. 3 .. 218-220(v.26), 224(v.29)

technique (see also practice, transcendental meditation), ch. 2 .. 117-122(v.39-41), 126-132(v.45), 162(v.61); ch. 3 .. 178 (intro.), 189-190(v.6-7), 194(v.9), 198(v.11), 201(v.13), 223(v.28), 239-240(v.39), 245(v.43); ch. 4 .. 255(v.2), 267 (v.11), 278(v.17), 305(v.35); ch. 5 .. 328(intro.), 340(v.7), 374(v.25); ch. 6 .. 384(intro.), 389(v.2), 409(v.13)

technique of teaching *Sankhya,* ch. 4 .. 275(v.16)

temptation, ch. 6 .. 463(v.44)

tension (see also stress and strain), ch. 2 .. 139(v.49), 156(v.57), 191-192(v.8); ch. 3 .. 239(v.39); ch. 5 .. 333(v.3)

'That thou art', ch. 2 .. 81(v.3); ch. 5 .. 357(v.17)

theoretical knowledge, ch. 4 .. 300-301(v.32); ch. 6 .. 466(v.46)

theory of action, ch. 3 .. 205(v.15)

thief, ch. 3 .. 199-200(v.12)

thinking (see also thought), ch. 1 .. 49(v.28), 53(v.29); ch. 2 .. 83(v.6), 140(v.49), 152(v.55); ch. 3 .. 183-185(v.3), 189 (v.6), 219(v.26); ch. 4 .. 282(v.19), 284(v.19), 303-304 (v.34), 320(v.41); ch. 5 .. 339(v.7); ch. 6 .. 390(v.3), 394 (v.4), 400(v.8), 411-412(v.14), 432-436(v.25-26), 443-444 (v.30), 448(v.32), 452(v.34)

thinking, code of, ch. 3 .. 186(v.3)

thinking, content of, ch. 3 .. 186(v.3)

thinking level (see also conscious thinking level), ch. 2 .. 140 (v.49), 152(v.55)

thinking of God, ch. 3 .. 185(v.3); ch. 5 .. 345(v.10); ch. 6 .. 444-445(v.30-31)

thinking of non-attachment, ch. 6 .. 386-387(v.1)

thinking of the divine Self, ch. 3 .. 185(v.3)

thinking process, inception of, ch. 2 .. 140(v.49)

thought (see also thinking), ch. 2 .. 141(v.49), 163(v.62), 169
(v.68); ch. 3 .. 213-214(v.20), 236(v.37), 241(v.40); ch. 4
.. 276(v.17), 282(v.19), 284(v.19), 291(v.24), 298(v.30),
309(v.36), 314-315(v.38); ch. 5 .. 326(intro.), 332(v.2),
342(v.8,9), 344-345(v.10); ch. 6 .. 389(v.3), 406(v.12),
409-411(v.14), 413(v.15), 418(v.18), 421-423(v.19-20),
430(v.24), 432-436(v.25-26), 441(v.28), 443-444(v.30),
447(v.31)

thought during transcendental meditation, ch. 6 .. 433-436(v.25-
26), 411(v.14)

thought, impulse of, ch. 4 .. 284(v.19)

thought, intensity of, ch. 6 .. 432(v.25)

thought, man of, ch. 3 .. 184(v.3); ch. 6 .. 389-393(v.3)

thought of action, ch. 3 .. 189(v.6)

thought of Being, ch. 5 .. 344-345(v.10)

thought, powerful, ch. 3 .. 214(v.20)

thought process, ch. 3 .. 219(v.26); ch. 6 .. 403-404(v.10), 406
(v.12)

thought, start of a, ch. 4 .. 282(v.19)

thought, subdued, ch. 6 .. 421-422(v.19)

thoughts, authorship of, ch. 6 .. 411(v.14)

thoughts, controlling, ch. 5 .. 375(v.26), 377(v.27)

thoughts, disciplined, ch. 2 .. 122-123(v.42); ch. 5 .. 374-376(v.26)

thoughts in meditation, ch. 6 .. 411(v.14)

three fields of faith, ch. 4 .. 316-317(v.39)

three gunas, ch. 2 .. 126-132(v.45-46), df. 128-129(v.45), 160
(v.59); ch. 3 .. 179(v.1), 188(v.5), 206(v.15), 219-226
(v.26-30), 228(v.32), 233-240(v.35-39); ch. 4 .. 251(v.1),
262(v.7), 269-270(v.13), 274(v.16), 279(v.18), 287(v.21-
22), 291(v.24), 296(v.27), 306-307(v.35), 311-312(v.38);
ch. 5 .. 330(v.1), 342(v.8,9), 352(v.14), 354(v.15), 357
(v.17), 374(v.25); ch. 6 .. 424(v.21)

three gunas, basis of the, ch. 3 .. 234(v.35); ch. 4 .. 270(v.13)

three gunas, dharma of the, ch. 3 .. 233-234(v.35)

three gunas, knowledge of, ch. 3 .. 222(v.28)

three prerequisites for success in Yoga, ch. 6 .. 454(v.36)

three prerequisites to cosmic consciousness, ch. 6 .. 438(v.27)

three states of silence, ch. 6 .. 392(v.3)

three worlds, ch. 3 .. 215-216(v.22)

time, ch. 1 .. 65(v.40); ch. 2 .. 99(v.20); ch. 4 .. 253-260(v.1-5), 273(v.15), 311(v.37), 315-316(v.38), 318(v.39); ch. 5 .. 335(v.5), 337(v.6); ch. 6 .. 421(v.19), 439(v.28), 465-466 (v.45-46)

time, Indian conception of, ch. 4 .. 252-255(v.1)

time, space and causation, ch. 4 .. 265(v.9); ch. 5 .. 339(v.7); ch. 6 .. 407(v.12)

tradition, ch. 1 .. 64-69(v.40-44); ch. 3 .. 192(v.8); ch. 4 .. 256-258(v.2-3), 260(v.6), 273(v.15); ch. 6 .. 384(v.1)

tradition, break away from, ch. 4 .. 256(v.2)

tradition, holy, ch. 4 .. 257-258(v.2-3)

tradition of Vedic wisdom, ch. 4 .. 256-257(v.2)

tradition, *Shankaracharya,* ch. 4 .. 256-257(v.2)

traditions, family, ch. 1 .. 66-69(v.42-44)

tranquility, ch. 2 .. 165(v.65)

transcend, ability to, ch. 3 .. 207(v.15)

transcend through worshipping, ch. 4 .. 293(v.25)

transcendental, ch. 2 .. 101(v.23), 103(v.25), 126(v.45)

transcendental consciousness (see also bliss-consciousness, Being, pure consciousness), ch. 2 .. 121(v.41), 126(v.45), 131 (v.45), 135-137(v.48), 142(v.50), 144-148(v.51-53), 151 (v.55), 153(v.55), 158-159(v.58), 160(v.59), 166-167(v.66), 173(v.72); ch. 3 .. 179(v.1), 183-186(v.3), 190(v.7), 194 (v.9), 196(v.10), 198(v.11), 201-202(v.13), 212(v.19), 223 (v.28), 225(v.30), 229(v.33); ch. 4 .. 266(v.10), 270(v.13), 282-283(v.19), 288-289(v.22-23), 293(v.25), 296(v.27), 301-302(v.32-33), 306(v.35), 309(v.36), 312-314(v.38), 316-317(v.39), 321(v.42); ch. 5 .. 327-328(intro.), 332-334(v.2-3), 337(v.6), 346-348(v.11), 357-358(v.17), 363-364(v.20-21), 369(v.23), 374(v.25); ch. 6 .. 387-397(v.1-5), 405(v.10), 407(v.12), 410-412(v.14), 418-419(v.18), 423-425(v.20-21), 429-431(v.24), 433-436(v.25-26), 440 (v.28), 452-453(v.34-35), 460(v.41), 463-466(v.44-46)

transcendental consciousness, means of gaining, ch. 3 .. 198(v.11)

transcendental consciousness to cosmic consciousness, transformation of, ch. 6 .. 429-441(v.24-28)

transcendental meditation (see also meditation, practice, technique), ch. 1 .. 44-45(v.23); ch. 2 .. 136-138(v.48), 141 (v.49), 144-145(v.51), 150-151(v.55), 155-156(v.56-57), 161-162(v.61), 166-167(v.66), 169(v.68), 172-173(v.71-72);

ch. 3 .. 178(intro.), 180(v.1), 185(v.3), 190(v.7), 192-194
(v.8,9), 198(v.11), 201(v.13), 205(v.14), 210-211(v.19),
214(v.20), 219-220(v.26-27), 223(v.28), 226(v.30); ch. 4 ..
266(v.10), 282(v.19), 289(v.23), 294-295(v.26-27), 298-
301(v.29-32), 312-314(v.38), 317(v.39), 319-320(v.40-41),
322(v.42); ch. 5 .. 326(intro.), 331-332(v.2), 335-336(v.4-
5), 340(v.7), 343-346(v.8-11), 360(v.19), 369(v.23), 371
(v.24), 374(v.25); ch. 6 .. 384(intro.), 386-387(v.1), 389-
390(v.2-3), 397(v.5), 400-414(v.8-15), 417(v.17), 428(v.23),
430(v.24), 434-436(v.25-26), 440(v.28), 445(v.30), 453
(v.35), 455(v.36), 457(v.38)

transcendental meditation, contrast during, ch. 6 .. 403(v.10)

transcendental meditation, discomfort during, ch. 6 .. 432(v.25)

transcendental meditation, distraction during, ch. 6 .. 436(v.26)

transcendental meditation, glory of, ch. 5 .. 344(v.8,9)

transcendental meditation, innocence in, ch. 6 .. 411(v.14), 432-
433(v.25)

transcendental meditation, intellectual analysis during, ch. 6 ..
433(v.25)

transcendental meditation, receptivity in, ch. 6 .. 433(v.25)

transcendental meditation, simplicity of (see also automatic, easy),
ch. 2 .. 117-120(v.40), 144(v.51); ch. 5 .. 377(v.27)

transcendental meditation, stopping, ch. 6 .. 457-461(v.38-41)

transcendental meditation, thought during, ch. 6 .. 411(v.14), 433-
436(v.25-26)

transcending, ch. 2 .. 129(v.45), 153(v.55), 162(v.61); ch. 3 ..
198(v.11), 207(v.15), 219(v.26), 224-225(v.29-30), 245
(v.43); ch. 4 .. 266(v.10), 279(v.18), 293(v.25), 299(v.31);
ch. 5 .. 338(v.7); ch. 6 .. 394(v.4), 403-404(v.10), 407
(v.12), 421-425(v.19-21), 432(v.25), 435(v.26), 437-438
(v.27), 443-444(v.30)

transformation of cosmic consciousness into God-consciousness,
ch. 4 .. 307(v.35), 313(v.38), 315(v.38); ch. 5 .. 348(v.11)

transformation of transcendental consciousness to cosmic consciousness, ch. 6 .. 429-441(v.24-28)

Treta-Yuga, ch. 4 .. 254(v.1)

trinity of experience, ch. 3 .. 206(v.15); ch. 6 .. 394(v.4)

truth, ch. 1 .. 65(v.40); ch. 2 .. 90(v.11), 96(v.16); ch. 4 .. 251
(v.1), 254(v.1), 256-258(v.2-3), 305(v.34), 317(v.39); ch.
5 .. 330(v.1), 335(v.5), 342(v.8,9), 367(v.22); ch. 6 ..
396(v.5), 411(v.14), 421(v.19), 441(v.28), 449(v.32)

trying to forget, ch. 6 .. 405(v.10)

turbulent senses, ch. 2 .. 161(v.60)

turiya (transcendental consciousness), ch. 3 .. 187(v.4)

twenty-four divisions, ch. 3 .. 222(v.28)

twice-born, ch. 1 .. 32(v.7)

two aspects of realization, ch. 6 .. 400(v.8)

two conditions for realization, ch. 5 .. 363(v.20)

two fullnesses, ch. 2 .. 79(v.2); ch. 4 .. 250-251(intro.), 256(v.2), 262(v.7), 279(v.18); ch. 6 .. 449(v.32)

two levels of function in the nervous system, ch. 4 .. 314-315 (v.38)

two paths of *Yoga,* ch. 3 .. 184-186(v.3)

two states of consciousness simultaneously, ch. 3 .. 226(v.30); ch. 4 .. 314-315(v.38); ch. 5 .. 362-363(v.20)

two states of Union, ch. 6 .. 449(v.32)

two types of people, ch. 3 .. 184-186(v.3); ch. 4 .. 294(v.26); ch. 5 .. 335(v.5)

two ways of life (see also householder, recluse), ch. 3 .. 184-186 (v.3); ch. 5 .. 335(v.5); ch. 6 .. 384-385(intro.-v.1)

twofold purpose of *Krishna,* ch. 4 .. 263-264(v.8)

uddharet (raise his self), ch. 6 .. 395(v.5)

unattached (see also detachment, non-attachment), ch. 2 .. 144 (v.57), 160(v.59); ch. 3 .. 210-212(v.19), 221-223(v.28); ch. 4 .. 283(v.19); ch. 5 .. 366(v.22), 369(v.23); ch. 6 .. 385(v.1)

unborn, ch. 2 .. 99-100(v.20-21); ch. 4 .. 260-161(v.6)

uncreated, ch. 5 .. 352(v.14)

understanding (see also intellectual understanding, knowledge), ch.2 .. 94-95(v.15), 116(v.39), 154-155(v.56); ch. 3 .. 228 (v.32); ch. 4 .. 249(intro.), 274-276(v.16-17), 280(v.18), 284(v.19), 304(v.34), 312(v.38), 320(v.41), 322(v.42); ch. 5 .. 334(v.4), 356(v.16), 375(v.26); ch. 6 .. 400-401 (v.8), 412(v.14), 442(v.29), 449(v.32), 452(v.34), 456(v.37)

understanding, intellectual (see also knowledge, understanding), ch. 2 .. 100(v.21), 103(v.25), 106-107(v.29), 116-117(v.39), 152(v.55); ch. 3 .. 177(intro.), 180(v.1), 185(v.3), 219 (v.26), 222-224(v.28-29), 227(v.31), 239(v.39); ch. 4 .. 274(v.16), 320(v.41); ch. 5 .. 363(v.20)

undeveloped intellect, ch. 5 .. 335(v.5)

undisciplined man, ch. 6 .. 454-455(v.36)

undue fondness, ch. 2 .. 155-157(v.57)

uninvolved state of intellect, ch. 2 .. 138(v.49)

Union (see also Unity), ch. 2 .. 116(v.39), 131(v.45), 135(v.48);
       ch. 3 .. 183(v.3), 199(v.12), 225(v.30); ch. 4 .. 273(v.15),
       278-279(v.17-18), 299(v.30), 307(v.35), 321(v.42); ch. 5 ..
       325(intro.), 327-328(intro.), 332-333(v.2), 337-338(v.6),
       342(v.8,9), 368(v.23), 370-371(v.23-24), 375(v.26); ch. 6 ..
       385(v.1), 391-393(v.3,4), 402(v.10), 412(v.14), 416(v.17),
       421-422(v.19), 426-428(v.22-23), 441(v.28), 445(v.30),
       447-450(v.32), 462(v.43), 467-468(v.47)

Union, fulfilment of, ch. 4 .. 321(v.42)

Union, mature state of, ch. 4 .. 321(v.42)

union of self and Self, ch. 5 .. 339-340(v.7)

Union, two states of, ch. 6 .. 449(v.32)

Union with Brahman, ch. 5 .. 364-366(v.21)

Union with God, ch. 3 .. 187(v.4); ch. 4 .. 266(v.10), 273(v.15);
       ch. 5 .. 379-380(v.29); ch. 6 .. 447-450(v.32)

Union with God, metaphysics of, ch. 6 .. 449(v.32)

united, ch. 2 .. 161-163(v.61); ch. 6 .. 418-420(v.18)

Unity (see also Union), ch. 2 .. 126(v.45), 137(v.48), 155(v.57);
       ch. 3 .. 177(intro.), 211(v.19); ch. 4 .. 251(intro.), 256
       (v.2), 272(v.14), 276(v.17), 301-302(v.32-33), 305-308
       (v.35), 312-313(v.38), 315-316(v.38), 318(v.39); ch. 5 ..
       327(intro.), 332(v.2), 336(v.5), 340(v.7), 347-348(v.11-
       12), 359(v.18), 370(v.23); ch. 6 .. 383(intro.), 391-392
       (v.3), 394(v.4), 412(v.14), 423(v.20), 426-427(v.22-23),
       436(v.26), 442-443(v.29-30), 445-449(v.31-32), 468(v.47)

Unity, living silence of, ch. 6 .. 391-392(v.3)

Unity of Self and activity, ch. 3 .. 193(v.8), 211(v.19); ch. 4 ..
       307(v.35); ch. 5 .. 332(v.2), 347(v.11)

Unity with the Divine, criterion of, ch. 5 .. 370(v.23)

universal love, ch. 3 .. 214(v.20); ch. 4 .. 307(v.35)

Universal Mother, ch. 4 .. 253(v.1)

universality (see also cosmic life), ch. 2 .. 97-98(v.17-18); ch. 3 ..
       188(v.5), 202(v.13); ch. 6 .. 396(v.5), 423(v.20), 426
       (v.23)

universality of activity, ch. 3 .. 188(v.5)

universe, conquer the, ch. 5 .. 360-361(v.19)

unmanifest (see also Absolute), ch. 2 .. 99(v.20), 102(v.25), 105-
       106(v.28-29), 213(v.20), 216(v.23); ch. 3 .. 216(v.23),
       236(v.37); ch. 4 .. 261(v.6)

unreal, ch. 2 .. 95-96(v.16)

unrighteous (see also sin), ch. 3 .. 200-203(v.13)

unshaken, ch. 2 .. 154-155(v.56)

upaiti (comes to), ch. 6 .. 437(v.27)

Upanishads, ch. 2 .. 81(v.3), 167(v.66); ch. 3 .. 195(v.9); ch. 4 .. 250(intro.), 256(v.2), 279(v.18); ch. 5 .. 355(v.16), 357 (v.17); ch. 6 .. 409(v.14), 437-438(v.27), 440(v.28), 443 (v.29), 449(v.32)

Upanishads, milk of the, ch. 6 .. 443(v.29)

Upasana Kanda (pertaining to the mind in relation to Reality), ch. 2 .. 123(v.42); ch. 3 .. 195(v.9)

upright action (see also right action), ch. 6 .. 459(v.40)

upward flow of energy, ch. 6 .. 410(v.14)

urdhvaretas (one whose energy flows only in an upward direction), ch. 6 .. 410(v.14)

validity of action, ch. 2 .. 114(v.38); ch. 3 .. 209-212(v.18-19), 215(v.22)

value of action, ch. 2 .. 140(v.49); ch. 4 .. 276(v.17)

value of events, ch. 4 .. 252(v.1)

values, ch. 2 .. 149(v.54), 155(v.56), 164(v.63-64); ch. 3 .. 199 (v.12), 217-218(v.24-26), 228(v.32); ch. 5 .. 343-344 (v.8,9); ch. 6 .. 453-454(v.35-36)

values, proper sense of, ch. 6 .. 453-454(v.35-36)

Varshneya, ch. 3 .. 235(v.36)

Veda, beyond the, ch. 6 .. 463(v.44)

Vedanta, ch. 2 .. 79(v.2); ch. 4 .. 256-257(v.2)

Vedas, ch. 1 .. 32(v.7), 67(v.42); ch. 2 .. 122-123(v.42-46), 147-148(v.53); ch. 3 .. 195(v.9), 197(v.11), 204-206(v.14-15); ch. 4 .. 256(v.2), 300-301(v.32); ch. 5 .. 359(v.18); ch. 6 .. 463(v.44)

Vedic rites, ch. 3 .. 194-195(v.9), 204(v.14); ch. 4 .. 297(v.28); ch. 6 .. 463(v.44)

Vedic wisdom, custodians of, ch. 4 .. 256(v.2)

Vedic wisdom, tradition of, ch. 4 .. 256-257(v.2)

vertical plane, ch. 2 .. 135(v.47)

vibrating consciousness, ch. 3 .. 236(v.37)

vibration, ch. 2 .. 111(v.34); ch. 3 .. 206(v.15), 236(v.37)

village of the senses, ch. 6 .. 429-431(v.24)

virtue (see also pious, righteousness), ch. 1 .. 61(v.36); ch. 5 .. 354(v.15), 356(v.16)

Vishnu, ch. 4 .. 253(v.1)

vision, ch. 5 .. 358-360(v.18), 367(v.22), 376-377(v.27); ch. 6 ..
    401(v.8), 441-442(v.29), 446(v.31), 448(v.32)
vision, evenness of, ch. 5 .. 359-360(v.18); ch. 6 .. 420(v.18),
    441-442(v.29), 447-448(v.32), 450(v.33)
vision in enlightenment, criterion of, ch. 5 .. 358-360(v.18)
Vyasa, ch. 1 .. 39(v.15), 46(v.24); ch. 4 .. 252-253(v.1)

waking state, ch. 2 .. 173-174(v.72); ch. 3 .. 184(v.3), 186-188
    (v.3-5), 193-194(v.9), 201(v.13), 208(v.17), 226(v.30);
    ch. 4 .. 277(v.17), 312-314(v.38), 316-317(v.39); ch. 5 ..
    338-340(v.7), 362-364(v.20-21), 367(v.22); ch. 6 .. 391
    (v.3), 415-416(v.16)
wandering mind, ch. 2 .. 117-121(v.39-41), 160(v.59), 166(v.66);
    ch. 5 .. 371(v.24); ch. 6 .. 413(v.15), 451-453(v.34-35)
want, feeling of (see also desire), ch. 4 .. 284(v.19)
war (see also battle, fight), ch. 1 .. 36(v.13), 45(v.23), 55(v.31),
    58(v.33); ch. 2 .. 85(v.5), 108(v.31)
warrior (see also *kshatriya*), ch. 1 .. 52(v.29), 71(v.46)
wavering intellect, ch. 2 .. 151(v.55)
wavering mind, ch. 6 .. 435-436(v.26), 450-453(v.33-35)
waves of influence, ch. 4 .. 276(v.17)
weakness, ch. 1 .. 46(v.25); ch. 2 .. 142(v.50), 163(v.62); ch. 4 ..
    257(v.2), 266(v.10), 318(v.40); ch. 6 .. 436(v.26)
weakness of mind, ch. 2 .. 78(v.2); ch. 6 .. 436(v.26)
weakness, source of, ch. 4 .. 318(v.40)
welfare of the world, ch. 3 .. 212-214(v.20), 217-218(v.25)
wheel of creation, ch. 3 .. 208(v.16)
wheel, revolving, ch. 3 .. 207-208(v.16)
will of God, ch. 6 .. 411(v.14)
wisdom, ch. 1 .. 49-52(v.28); ch. 3 .. 238-241(v.39-40); ch. 5 ..
    354-359(v.15-18), 361(v.19), 376(v.26), 379-380(v.29);
    ch. 6 .. 443(v.30), 459(v.39), 461(v.42)
wise man (see also great man, integrated man, realized man), ch.
    3 .. 217-220(v.25-26); ch. 5 .. 359(v.18)
withdrawal from life, ch. 6 .. 405(v.10)
withdrawal of the senses, ch. 2 .. 158-159(v.58), 168-169(v.68)
without foothold, ch. 6 .. 457-458(v.38)
without possessions, ch. 6 .. 402-405(v.10)
witness, ch. 2 .. 98(v.19); ch. 4 .. 291(v.24); ch. 5 .. 350(v.13),
    354(v.15)
women, ch. 1 .. 65-66(v.41)

word, ch. 3 .. 198(v.11)

world, welfare of the, ch. 3 .. 212-214(v.20), 217-218(v.25)

worldly desires, ch. 2 .. 151(v.55)

worlds of the righteous, ch. 6 .. 460-461(v.41)

worship, ch. 4 .. 257(v.2), 292-293(v.25); ch. 6 .. 445-448(v.31-32), 467-468(v.47)

worshipping, transcend through, ch. 4 .. 293(v.25)

wrong (see also sin, wrong action), ch. 1 .. 63(v.39); ch. 2 .. 114(v.38), 127-130(v.45); ch. 5 .. 345(v.10)

wrong action (see also right and wrong, sin, wrong), ch. 1 .. 44 (v.23); ch. 3 .. 191(v.8), 207(v.15), 220(v.26); ch. 4 .. 276-277(v.17), 308-309(v.36)

wrong-doing (see also wrong action), ch. 1 .. 44(v.23); ch. 4 .. 262(v.7), 309(v.36)

yagya (action which helps evolution), ch. 3 .. 193-207(v.9-15), df. 194(v.9), df. 204(v.14); ch. 4 .. 288-303(v.23-33), df. 299(v.31); ch. 5 .. 379(v.29)

yagya, advantages of, ch. 3 .. 196-198(v.10-11)

yagya, automatic, ch. 3 .. 198(v.11)

yagya, complete conception of, ch. 3 .. 206(v.15)

yagya, eat the remains of, ch. 3 .. 200-203(v.13); ch. 4 .. 299(v.31)

yagya, fruits of, ch. 4 .. 301(v.32)

yagya, fundamental, ch. 3 .. 201(v.13)

yagya, goal of, ch. 3 .. 201(v.13); ch. 4 .. 301-302(v.32-33)

yagya, gross aspect of, ch. 3 .. 195(v.9), 205(v.14)

yagya, knowledge of, ch. 4 .. 301(v.32)

yagya of knowledge, ch. 4 .. 301-303(v.33)

yagya of material means, ch. 4 .. 302-303(v.33)

yagya, remains of, ch. 3 .. df. 200-201(v.13)

yagya, subtle aspect of, ch. 3 .. 195(v.9), 205(v.14)

yagyas and austerities, enjoyer of, ch. 5 .. 379(v.29)

Yoga, ch. 2 .. 116-122(v.39-41), 135-149(v.48-54), 174(v.72); ch. 3 .. 177(intro.), 179(v.1), 183-186(v.3), 204(v.14), 223(v.28); ch. 4 .. 249-258(intro.-v.3), 260(v.6), 295-297 (v.27-28), 311-317(v.38-39), 319-322(v.41-42); ch. 5 .. 325 (intro.), 327-329(intro.-v.1), 332(v.2), 334-338(v.3-7), 356 (v.16-17), 361(v.19), 363(v.20), 373-374(v.25-26), 376 (v.26); ch. 6 .. 384(intro.), 388-394(v.2-4), 406-407(v.12), 414-418(v.16-17), 422-424(v.19-20), 426-429(v.22-24), 441-442(v.29), 450(v.33), 454-456(v.36-37), 460-461(v.41), 463-464(v.44-45), 466(v.46)

Yoga, aim of (see also goal of *Yoga*), ch. 3 .. 177(intro.)

Yoga and renunciation, relationship of, ch. 5 .. 331(v.1); ch. 6 .. 385-389(v.1-2)

Yoga and *Sankhya,* relationship of, ch. 5 .. 335-336(v.4-5), 355-356(v.16-17), 366(v.21)

Yoga, aspirant to, ch. 6 .. 463(v.44)

Yoga, definition of, ch. 6 .. 422-428(v.19-23)

Yoga, essence of, ch. 2 .. 126-138(v.45-48)

Yoga, established in, ch. 2 .. 135-138(v.48); ch. 6 .. 441-443(v.29)

Yoga, fire of, ch. 4 .. 295-296(v.27)

Yoga, glory of, ch. 6 .. 426(v.22)

Yoga, goal of, ch. 2 .. 118(v.40), 147(v.53); ch. 6 .. 453(v.35)

Yoga, loss of, ch. 4 .. 255-256(v.2)

Yoga, not perfected in, ch. 6 .. 455-457(v.37)

Yoga of action (see also *Karma Yoga*), ch. 3 .. 183-186(v.3), 189-190(v.7); ch. 5 .. 328-336(intro.-v.5), 365(v.21), 373(v.25)

Yoga of knowledge, ch. 3 .. 183-186(v.3)

Yoga of renunciation, ch. 5 .. 327-328(intro.), 365(v.21)

Yoga, proper means of gaining, ch. 6 .. 454-455(v.36)

Yoga, purpose of, ch. 6 .. 428(v.23)

Yoga Shastra (Scripture of *Yoga*), ch. 3 .. 199(v.12), 233(v.35); ch. 4 .. 278(v.17)

Yoga, success in the practice of, ch. 6 .. 415(v.16), 454(v.36)

Yoga, two paths of, ch. 3 .. 184-186(v.3)

Yoga, three prerequisites for success in, ch. 6 .. 454(v.36)

yogastah kuru karmani (established in *Yoga,* perform action), ch. 2 .. 138(v.49); ch. 3 .. 177(intro.)

yogi, ch. 2 .. 86(v.7); ch. 4 .. 292-293(v.25); ch. 5 .. 345-348 (v.11), df. 346(v.11), 370-372(v.23-24); ch. 6 .. 384-389 (v.1-2), 392(v.3), 400-414(v.8-15), 421-423(v.19-20), 437-441(v.27-28), 445-450(v.31-32), 464-468(v.45-47)

yogi, accomplished, ch. 6 .. 402(v.10)

yogi, criteria of, ch. 2 .. 148-174(v.54-72); ch. 6 .. 384-389(v.1-2)

yogi, highest, ch. 6 .. 447-450(v.32)

yogi, superiority of a, ch. 6 .. 465-466(v.46)

yogis, family of, ch. 6 .. 461(v.42)

Yogishvara (Lord of the *Yogis*), ch. 5 .. 328(intro.)

Yuga, ch. 4 .. 254(v.1)

INDEX OF ANALOGIES

aeroplane, catching an, ch. 5 .. 362(v.20)

amnion, ch. 3 .. 238(v.38)

anchor and ship, ch. 2 .. 129(v.45); ch. 5 .. 369(v.23)

arrow and bow, ch. 2 .. 136(v.48), 140(v.49), 141-142(v.50);
    ch. 4 .. 300(v.31)

boat, ch. 2 .. 164(v.63); ch. 3 .. 182(v.2)

boats in fast current, ch. 1 .. 66(v.41)

body and limbs, ch. 1 .. 68(v.43)

bow and arrow, ch. 2 .. 136(v.48), 140(v.49), 141-142(v.50);
    ch. 4 .. 300(v.31)

branches and trunk, ch. 4 .. 256(v.2)

bread, ch. 6 .. 444(v.30)

brothers, ch. 6 .. 398(v.6)

bubble, 470 (appendix)

business man, ch. 2 .. 117(v.39), 127(v.45), 136-137(v.48), 142
    (v.50)

cells, ch. 3 .. 197-198(v.11)

chariot, ch. 1 .. 36(v.14)

children's toys, ch. 2 .. 157(v.57); ch. 6 .. 446(v.31), 449(v.32)

cloth, dyeing, ch. 4 .. 313(v.38); ch. 6 .. 462(v.43)

cloth, washing, ch. 6 .. 459(v.40)

coconut, ch. 5 .. 351(v.14)

crown prince, ch. 6 .. 425(v.21)

currents of water, ch. 3 .. 242(v.41)

darkness and light, ch. 2 .. 119-120(v.40), 126(v.45), 170(v.69);
    ch. 3 .. 244(v.43); ch. 4 .. 309(v.36), 317(v.39); ch. 5 ..
    355(v.16); ch. 6 .. 424(v.20), 433(v.25)

diving, ch. 2 .. 119(v.40), 136(v.48), 145(v.51)

dog, disciplining a, ch. 6 .. 454-455(v.36)

dust, ch. 3 .. 238(v.38)

dyeing cloth, ch. 4 .. 313(v.38); ch. 6 .. 462(v.43)

embryo, ch. 3 .. 238(v.38)

enemy, ch. 5 .. 341(v.7)

energy (physics), ch. 2 .. 105(v.28); ch. 6 .. 440(v.28)

fire, ch. 3 .. 194(v.9), 236(v.37), 238(v.38); ch. 4 .. 282(v.19)
First English Reader, ch. 3 .. 232(v.35)

garments, ch. 2 .. 100(v.22)
glasses, ch. 5 .. 367(v.22)
government, ch. 4 .. 262(v.7)
green spectacles, ch. 4 .. 306(v.35); ch. 6 .. 446(v.31)

honey, ch. 4 .. 285(v.20)

king, ch. 2 .. 95(v.15); ch. 6 .. 425(v.21)

lamp, ch. 6 .. 421-422(v.19)
leaf, ch. 2 .. 78(v.2)
light, ch. 2 .. 121(v.40)
light and darkness, ch. 2 .. 119-120(v.40), 126(v.45), 170(v.69);
    ch. 3 .. 244(v.43); ch. 4 .. 309(v.36), 317(v.39); ch. 5 ..
    355(v.16); ch. 6 .. 424(v.20), 433(v.25)
limbs and body, ch. 1 .. 68(v.43)

man on mountain peak, ch. 2 .. 122(v.41)
millionaire, ch. 2 .. 136-137(v.48), 154(v.56)
mirror, ch. 3 .. 238(v.38)
mother and child, ch. 2 .. 95(v.15)
mountain, ch. 3 .. 242(v.41)
music, ch. 2 .. 118(v.40)

ocean, ch. 1 .. 58(v.34), 63(v.39); ch. 2 .. 94(v.15), 170-171
    (v.70); ch. 3 .. 240(v.39); ch. 4 .. 260(v.5); ch. 5 .. 341
    (v.7); ch. 6 .. 422(v.19); appendix, 470
ocean and river, ch. 2 .. 171(v.70)
officer, ch. 3 .. 243(v.42)
orange, ch. 2 .. 77-78(v.1); ch. 3 .. 206-207(v.15)
oxygen and hydrogen, ch. 4 .. 270(v.13); appendix, 471

patient and surgeon, ch. 2 .. 85(v.7)
physics (energy), ch. 2 .. 105(v.28)
pleasing melody, ch. 2 .. 118(v.40)
poor man and wealthy man, ch. 2 .. 156(v.57)

reflection, ch. 2 .. 166(v.66)

reservoir, ch. 2 .. 132(v.46)

retail merchant, ch. 5 .. 367(v.22)

roasted seeds, ch. 4 .. 311(v.37)

root, watering the, ch. 2 .. 78(v.2); ch. 3 .. 245(v.43)

sap, ch. 4 .. 261(v.6); ch. 5 .. 360(v.19)

ship, ch. 2 .. 129(v.45), 167(v.67)

son of wealthy man, ch. 2 .. 137(v.48)

student, ch. 2 .. 134(v.47)

sun, ch. 2 .. 96(v.17), 119-120(v.40), 166(v.66); ch. 4 .. 309
      (v.36), 317(v.39); ch. 5 .. 341(v.7), 355(v.16); ch. 6 ..
      396(v.5)

sun and wind, ch. 6 .. 396(v.5)

surgeon, ch. 4 .. 261(v.6)

surgeon and patient, ch. 2 .. 85(v.7)

swimming, ch. 2 .. 136(v.48)

sword, ch. 4 .. 322(v.42)

thief, ch. 3 .. 200(v.12)

toys, ch. 2 .. 157(v.57); ch. 6 .. 446(v.31), 449(v.32)

tree, ch. 3 .. 245(v.43)

trunk and branches, ch. 4 .. 256(v.2)

vacuum, ch. 3 .. 220(v.27)

village, villager and landlord, ch. 6 .. 430(v.24)

walking, ch. 2 .. 129(v.45)

washing a cloth, ch. 6 .. 459(v.40)

water, ch. 2 .. 118(v.40), 166(v.66); ch. 4 .. 267(v.11), 311
      (v.38); ch. 6 .. 422(v.19)

water the root, ch. 2 .. 78(v.2); ch. 4 .. 277-278(v.17)

waves, ch. 1 .. 63(v.39); ch. 3 .. 240(v.39); ch. 4 .. 260(v.5);
      ch. 6 .. 422(v.19), 436(v.26), appendix, 470

wealthy man and poor man, ch. 2 .. 156(v.57)

wealthy man's son, ch. 2 .. 137(v.48)

whirlpool, ch. 3 .. 236(v.37)

white, ch. 1 .. 37(v.14)

white horses, ch. 1 .. 37(v.14)

wind and sun, ch. 6 .. 396(v.5)